"Wise's short book r............ .... polemic: Thomas Paine's *Common Sense* for the 21st century. . . . A post-racial United States is an imagined country."
—*Washington Post*

"Wise, a white anti-racism activist and scholar (and author of *White Like Me*), pushes plenty of buttons in this methodical breakdown of racism's place in the wake of Barack Obama's victory. . . . There's no sugar coating here for whites, nor are there any news flashes for Americans of color, but Wise bravely enumerates the unpalatable truths of a nation still struggling to understand its legacy of racist oppression."
—*Publishers Weekly*

"Wise outlines . . . how racism and white privilege have morphed to fit the modern social landscape. In prose that reads like his lightning-rod speeches, he draws from a long list of high-profile campaign examples to define what he calls 'Racism 2.0,' a more insidious form of racism that actually allows for and celebrates the achievements of individual people of color because they're seen as the exceptions, not the rules."—*Colorlines*

"This book makes an intriguing argument and is packed with insight. Wise clearly explains the complexity of institutional racism in contemporary society. He continuously reminds the reader that Obama's victory *may* signal the entrenchment of a more complicated, subtle, and insidious form of racism. The jury is still out."—*Multicultural Review*

"Tim Wise has looked behind the curtain. In *Between Barack and a Hard Place* he explores the real issues of race in the Obama campaign and incoming presidency, issues that the mainstream media has chosen to ignore. His book debunks any notion that the United States has entered a post-racial period; instead he identifies the problems that emerge in the context of the victory of a black presidential candidate who chose to run an essentially non-racial campaign. With this book, Wise hits the bull's eye."—Bill Fletcher Jr., Executive Editor of *BlackCommentator.com* and co-founder of the Center for Labor Renewal

"Tim Wise is one of the most brilliant, articulate and courageous critics of white privilege in the nation. His considerable rhetorical skills, his fluid literary gifts and his relentless search for the truth make him a critical ally in the fight against racism and a true soldier in the war for social justice. His writing and thinking constitute a bulwark of common sense, and uncommon wisdom, on the subject of race, politics and culture. He is a national treasure."—Michael Eric Dyson, Professor, Georgetown University, and best-selling author of more than a dozen books on race

"(Wise's) work is revolutionary, and those who react negatively are simply afraid of hearing the truth." —Robin D.G. Kelley, Professor of History, University of Southern California, author of *Thelonious Monk* and *Yo' Mama's Disfunktional!*

"Tim Wise is one of those rare 'public intellectuals' that numerous authors have suggested are becoming extinct in this society. He is evidence that this is not the case . . . . in my judgment, he is the very best of the white anti-racism writers and commentators working in the U.S. media today."—Joe Feagin, Graduate Research Professor of Sociology, Texas A&M, and author of more than twenty books on race issues

Dear White America

Dear White America

Letter to a New Minority

Tim Wise

CITY LIGHTS BOOKS
San Francisco

Cover design: Pollen

Library of Congress Cataloging-in-Publication Data
Wise, Tim J.
  Dear white America : letter to a new minority / Tim Wise.
     p. cm. — (City Lights Open Media)
   ISBN 978-0-87286-521-1 (pbk.)
1. Whites—Race identity—United States—History.
2. Whites—United States—Attitudes—History. 3. Social sta-
tus—United States—History. 4. Minorities—United States—
History. 5. Multiculturalism—United States—History. I. Title.
 E184.A1W573 2012
 305.809—dc23
                            2011034672

City Lights Books are published at the City Lights Bookstore,
261 Columbus Avenue, San Francisco, CA 94133.
www.citylights.com

NOTE TO THE READER

Believe me, I know there is something more than a little pretentious about penning a letter to what amounts to roughly 200 million people.

To begin, I realize that only a tiny fraction of that number will ever read it or learn of its existence. Of those, a disproportionate percentage will be persons who likely hold views similar to my own. Such is the nature of ideological polemic. It tends to find readership amongst those already predisposed to agree with the bulk of its contents, thereby missing the vast throngs of others who could perhaps benefit from those contents but will studiously avoid them precisely because they can tell—perhaps from the title or the jacket blurbs, or because they are already familiar with the author—that they won't likely agree with much of what lies inside.

I also recognize that by aiming said polemic at a group as vast and diverse as "white America," I will likely be accused of overreach. After all, how can one speak at once to 200 million people called white in this nation, who lead lives that vary based on geography, class status, gender, sexuality, religious affiliation, political ideology, and any number of other identity categories? Doesn't such an effort overgeneralize about white people, suggesting that there are things they all need to think about, are not thinking about now, and on which I am qualified to lecture?

Perhaps. But despite these caveats, I believe this effort to be a valuable one. First, even if most who read this letter are already of a progressive, liberal or left orientation, the contents may still be of assistance in conversations with others of decidedly different persuasions. We all have people in our lives with whom it can be difficult to talk about political matters, and especially when those matters touch on the always explosive topic of race, as this volume does. If my words may in some way strengthen your own, and allow you to more confidently discuss racial subjects with those difficult co-workers, relatives, neighbors, or friends, all the better. Sometimes efforts such as this are aimed less at those one seeks to "convert" than at those with whom one already sojourns in general agreement, but who need reinforcement for the struggle. Not to mention, those who make up the so-called "choir" are often not singing on key, certainly not nearly so much as they believe themselves to be. As a lifelong Southerner who has been around my fair share of choirs, I can say without fear of contradiction that choirs need practice.

Likewise, although I know there is great diversity among those of us called white, I also know that to be white, regardless of the many additional identities we may possess, *means something*. It matters, and has always mattered, throughout our nation's history. Despite our differences, there are certain aspects of the white American experience that are broadly similar. As I argued in my memoir, *White Like Me*, although we are—as with snowflakes—all different, we also must admit that (as with snowflakes) there are some general consistencies in our life trajectories that bind us together. We know snowflakes, after all, when we see them, and can make some statements about their experiences that are likely to be pretty close to the mark, regardless of whatever individual differences may exist between them: so too with persons defined as members of the same so-called race.

I also know that any time one takes aim at white folks over the subject of racism, as I do herein, one runs the risk of being accused of "hating" white people. It's a refrain that has been directed at me for years by those who find it difficult to differentiate between a critique of white racism and institutional white supremacy on the one hand, and of white people, as *people*, on the other. But there is a difference between these things. There have always been white people who have fought white racism and white supremacy as an institutional force, and there have always been people of color, for that matter, who have collaborated with it. This critique is less about people and more about mindsets; it is less about white people and more about *whiteness* as a social and institutional force—a social category created for the purpose of enshrining a racially divided polity. To condemn the latter is not to condemn the former.

Indeed, I find it ironic that one would assume issuing a critique of white racism and privilege was tantamount to hating whites. After all, to make such a claim suggests a dangerous and disturbing equation whereby, in effect, to love white people would require compliance with—if not a tacit *endorsement* of—white racism and privilege. But surely that is not what those who confuse my words with racial hatred would wish to suggest, is it? So no, I do not hate white people. I hate neither myself nor my wife, my two daughters, my parents, my best friend, his wife, their child or the elderly lady across the street, all of whom are white. It is out of a belief that white folks can and must do better—a belief that springs from a place of hopefulness, compassion, and even love—that I offer these thoughts.

And please note, this letter is not merely an outwardly directed missive, intended to scold others for their shortcomings where race is concerned. Throughout the letter I will often use the words "we" and "us" when referring to whites, because I know that many of these failings are mine too. Even those of us who have chosen the path of antiracist allyship, and who "get it" in many ways, still make mistakes regularly, fall into old patterns and inadvertently collaborate with the injustices we oppose. This letter is as much a self-reminder as anything else.

Additionally, although this letter is addressed to my fellow white Americans, my intention is for it to be of interest to all, including persons of color. For years, black and brown folks have told me that they needed to know what white folks were saying about race when people of color weren't around; further, they've asked for insights into the way white folks are thinking about race, which they often believe can best be provided by a well-placed insider, someone who speaks the language and knows the handshake, so to speak. Herein I try to offer some of those insights, and I hope they will prove instructive.

Because this volume is presented as a letter, I have opted to forego a traditional footnote style for the text. Inserting numerical notes in the body of the narrative might have proved distracting for readers, making the volume feel more like an academic work than a conversational letter. But because it is important to provide sources for various data claims and news references, I have included a notes section at the end of the text. There, you will find sources provided, with reference to the page number and passage to which the source refers.

Dear White America,

I have to confess to a longstanding fantasy, the fulfillment of which I resist, partly because of its impracticality, but also (and mostly) out of a general distaste for inviting violence upon my person. It typically comes to mind about the same time every year—at the very moment, in fact, that I find myself typing out these words—as cities and towns across the United States gear up for their respective Fourth of July celebrations, replete with fireworks, hot dogs, and lots of red, white and blue banners and flags assaulting the visual landscape from sea to shining sea.

In the fantasy, it's incredibly hot out, even as the daytime sun recedes, soon to give way to the darkening skies that will serve as the canvas for a colorful explosion of incendiary art: the end product of two unstoppable forces—American self-love and Chinese manufacturing—brought together in an audacious display of grandiosity.

As Lee Greenwood's "Proud to Be an American" blares from a sound system loaded onto the back of a truck and the yearly Independence Day parade begins, I bide my time. Then, just as the first procession of Boy Scouts passes, I turn to the man standing next to me, the one with the big "God Bless the USA" button on his hat, and ask: "Why can't you just get over it? I mean, why do you insist on living in the past? That whole 'breaking away from the British' thing was like more than 200 years ago. Isn't it time to *move on*?"

Then, before my stunned and increasingly belligerent target can manage to slug me for my apparent apostasy on this, the holiest of all national holidays, I break into a flat-out sprint, hurtling down the block. He gives chase, of course, but having consumed one too many pieces of Mom's apple pie, he becomes winded, ultimately giving up, shaking his fists and calling me names, before getting back to the orgy of Americanism in which he had been engaged prior to my arrival.

Please know that I'm not a sadistic type. I don't actually seek to cause distress, be it physical or emotional, to anyone, even to the kind of person who truly believes, against all visual evidence to the contrary, that the colors Betsy Ross sewed into that flag so long ago make for an acceptable wardrobe palette. It's just that every now and then I remember how quick so many of us are to use a similar line, and I feel as though we should perhaps be required to consider how it feels: all that judgmental arrogance and dismissiveness.

This is, after all, the common response that so many of our people offer whenever someone of color dares to mention the less than celebratory aspects of our national history: you know, like some of the parts involving *them*; especially the parts concerning the multiple centuries of human trafficking and racial subordination to which they were subjected, and from which we benefited, at least in relative terms. Indeed, whenever someone deigns to mention any of those matters—like the national legacy of enslavement, Indian genocide and imperialistic land grabs—the rebuttal to which we so often retreat is as automatic as it is enraging: "Oh, that was a long time ago, get over it," or "Stop living in the past," or "At some point, we just have to move on."

In other words, the past is the past, and we shouldn't dwell on it. Unless of course we *should* and indeed insist on doing so, as with the above-referenced Independence Day spectacle, or as many used to do with their cries of "Remember the Alamo" or "Remember Pearl Harbor." Both of those refrains, after all, took as their jumping-off point the rather obvious notion that the past does matter and should be remembered— a logic that apparently vanishes like early morning fog on a hot day when applied to the historical moments we'd rather forget. Not because they are any less historic, it should be noted, but merely because they are considerably less *convenient*.

Oh, and not to put too fine a point on it, but when millions of us have apparently chosen to affiliate ourselves with a political movement known as the Tea Party, which group's public rallies prominently feature some among us clothed in Revolutionary War costumes, wearing powdered wigs and carrying muskets, we are really in no position to lecture *anyone* about the importance of living in the present and getting past the past. All the less so when the rallying cry of that bunch appears to be that they seek to "take their country back." *Back*, after all, is a directional reference that points by definition to the past, so we ought to understand when some insist we should examine that past in its entirety, and not just the parts that many of us would rather remember.

Truth is, we love living in the past when it venerates this nation and makes us feel good. If the past allows us to reside in an idealized, mythical place, from which we can look down upon the rest of humanity as besotted inferiors who are no doubt jealous of our national greatness and our freedoms (*that*, of course, is why they hate us and why some attack us), then the past is the perfect companion: an old friend or lover, or at least a well-worn and reassuring shoe.

If, on the other hand, some among us insist that the past is more than that—if we point out that the past is also one of brutality, and that this brutality, especially as regards race, has mightily skewed the distribution of wealth and opportunity even to this day—then the past becomes a trifle, a pimple on the ass of *now*, an unwelcome reminder that although the emperor may wear clothes, the clothes he wears betray a shape he had rather hoped to conceal. No, no: the past, in those cases, is to be forgotten.

Vast numbers of us, it appears, would prefer to hermetically seal the past away in some memory vault, only peering inside on those occasions when it suits us and supports the cause of uncritical nationalism to which so many of us find ourselves imperviously wedded. But to treat the past this way is to engage in a fundamentally dishonest enterprise, one that, in the long run (as we'll see), is dangerous. Unless we grapple with the past in its fullness—and come to appreciate the impact of that past on our present moment—we will find it increasingly difficult to move into the future a productive, confident and even remotely democratic republic.

∞

But before we go any further, I realize that many of you reading this letter may not be comfortable being addressed in the collective sense—as *white America*. While we are quite used to referring to black folks and other people of color in terms of their group identity, we insist on referring to ourselves individually, almost as if to suggest that we lacked a racial identity, or that if we possess one, it contains no relevance to our lives. "I'm not *white*," some of you may say, "I'm just an *American*." Those are easy words to mouth when you've always been able to take your Americanness, your citizenship and your belonging for granted. Or better still, some say, "I'm not white, I'm just Bill," or "Suzie" or "Tom" or "Mary" or whatever one's name might be.

And yet, though we may prefer to deny it, I know that there *is* such a thing as white America. I know it because I am white myself, and have lived a life that has been intensely racialized. It's an experience that I doubt seriously is mine alone. From where I grew up, to the schools I attended, to the jobs I had, to the way I have been treated by authority figures—be they teachers, employers or cops—most everything about my experience has been at least partially (often significantly) related to my racial identity. So even though everyone is different, being white in America has meant something, just as being black, Latino, Asian or an indigenous person has meant something. History happened, and it matters.

From nearly the second that Europeans first stepped onto the shores of this continent, our identity mattered. It allowed us to feel superior to the native peoples whom we began to kill, subordinate and displace from their land almost immediately. It allowed us to take advantage of land-giveaway programs in the colonies—which we created, of course—like the headright system, which provided fifty acres of land to males from England who were willing to settle in the so-called New World. Within a few decades, classification as a white person would become the key to avoiding enslavement; it would determine who could hold office, who could sit on juries, who had rights of due process; and by the time the republic was founded, being considered white would become the key to citizenship itself. The Naturalization Act of 1790— the first law passed by Congress after the ratification of the Constitution—made clear that all white persons and *only* white persons could be considered citizens of the United States, a status that would elevate even the lowliest and most despised European ethnic above *all* persons of color, without exception, for generations to come.

Of course, even after the legal right to buy, sell, breed and enslave people of color officially ended, our whiteness continued to matter. It determined where one could live, work and attend school; it determined who would and would not have access to land and other wealth-building assets. Segregation and immigration restrictions aimed specifically at non-Europeans continued to make a mockery of our national pretense to freedom and democracy for another century after the fall of the chattel system. This nation was, simply put, conceived in and plagued by formal white supremacy for over 350 years, going back to the colonial period: it was a system of racial fascism. I know we don't like that kind of talk. It probably seems like the kind of thing that would only be said by someone who hated America, or, alternately, had studied history. Same thing, I guess, to some of us.

In any event, the reason I bring this up is not just to make a point about the past, but rather to frame the remarks that follow, because the past matters, and not merely as a historical referent. The past affects the present. Inertia is not merely a property of the physical universe; it also relates to the political, socioeconomic and cultural universe. We have to deal with the past because the past comes into the present whether we like it or not, and whether or not we wish to speak of it. It is akin to dirty laundry, and while I know that none of us likes to air such a thing in front of others, what I also know is that dirty laundry never manages to air itself.

Please understand that I don't wish for us to examine these matters so as to generate some kind of self-flagellating guilt on our part. I know we aren't to blame for history—either its horrors or the legacy it has left us. But we are responsible for how we bear that legacy, and what we make of it in the present. There is a difference, and it is not a small one, between guilt and responsibility, however much and however long we may have confused the two concepts, treating them simply as synonyms. Guilt is what you feel for the things you have done, while responsibility is what you take because of the kind of person you are. In any number of situations we take responsibility for things even when we were not, strictly speaking, directly to blame for them. So, for instance, we contribute tax dollars to remedy the effects of pollution, even when we have not, individually, released toxic waste into the air, soil and water. And surely, were we to become the CEO of a multibillion-dollar company, we would not be free to make use of the company's assets (all of which were accumulated before we got there, and for which we would be due no credit), while refusing to make payments on outstanding debts, just because we had not, ourselves, incurred them.

In the discussion about race and racism, to make note of the accumulated inequities, which date back generations, is not to blame anyone currently alive for those inequities. It is not intended to produce guilt, for indeed no one living today is directly responsible for them. But their legacy persists in many of today's institutions for which we are responsible. And just as we have inherited many of the blessings and national assets of past generations—the accumulated national wealth for instance—we have inherited the deficits too. To take advantage of the upside of history while refusing to address the downside—to make use of accumulated assets while refusing to take aim at the debts—would be morally irresponsible .

Don't misunderstand; I am not claiming that *all* the responsibility for fixing our nation's racial quandary rests with whites. Everyone has played a part in the mess, and everyone will need to be involved in digging out from under it. As my friend and colleague Jacqui Wade puts it, "We all have a few nickels in the quarter." But as a white person, I believe I have a responsibility—we all do—to clean up our own backyards, so to speak, before casting about for black and brown folks on whom to place blame for one or another aspect of our current crisis. It's called "personal responsibility," which, notably, is a term we use quite often when talking about people of color. We are quick to lecture *them* about the need to take personal responsibility for their lives, to stop blaming others or the system for their problems, to address the issues in their own communities, rather than deflecting blame onto us or the larger society we share. This is why we responded so favorably to the words of Bill Cosby several years ago, when he hectored black America to straighten up and address its own internal pathologies. But we seem unable or unwilling to apply the logic of personal responsibility to ourselves. We use it as a weapon against others, never noting the irony that to point at someone *else* while speaking of taking *personal* responsibility for oneself is the ultimate contradiction.

Of course people of color need to take personal responsibility for their lives and do whatever they can—regardless of circumstance, regardless of racism—to better their own situations. That has always been true, even under periods of formal apartheid. But that says nothing about what the larger society must do to improve the opportunity structures in which such persons must operate. Just because a person should work hard and behave responsibly, that does not mean the rest of us have no obligation to ensure a fair and just society within which that first person will be trying to better his or her station. Personal responsibility and collective responsibility are not mutually exclusive; rather, they are each contributory to the whole.

So while black and brown folks have work to do too, it is not *my* job, or yours, to dictate the terms of that effort. Nor can we suggest that until *they* do their part to make things better, *we* can remain inactive when it comes to doing ours. Each of us has a responsibility to do what we can, no matter what others do or don't do. If racism and institutionalized white advantage never went away, people of color would still have a moral obligation to do their best and to try their hardest; likewise, if people of color continue to do certain things from time to time that we feel only perpetuate their own disadvantage, we will still have an obligation to help create equity and end racial discrimination against them.

∞

The truth is, discrimination and inequity stalk the present day. In other words, it is not merely a matter of historical significance, but also a contemporary reality. Perhaps if the injuries and injustices of the past had been wiped away we could avoid this discussion, or at least relegate it to our history classes, but they haven't been, and so we can't. And this is yet another way I know you must exist, white America: because the data very clearly tell me that you do—that *we* do.

For instance, the data tell me that even before the present economic meltdown (which has only made things worse), our families possessed about twelve times the net worth of the typical black family and eight times that of the typical Latino family. Even black and brown middle-class families with good incomes and occupational status tended to have one-third to one-fifth the net worth of similar families in our communities. Now, in the wake of the collapsed economy, the median net worth among white families is *twenty times* that of black families and eighteen times greater than that of Latino families—a difference of over $100,000, between the typical white family and the typical family of color.

In large part those gaps were (and still are) the historical residue of generations of unequal opportunity and access. They certainly have nothing to do with superior investment wisdom on our parts. After all, if we have learned anything in the past few years of financial collapse, surely we should have learned this: a handful of rich white men—some of the best and brightest Wall Street has to offer—can lose a *hell of a lot of money* with no help from black folks, Mexicans (documented or not), Asian Americans or native peoples. In the course of only about eighteen months from 2007 to early 2009, these financial wizards—who possess no talent to produce anything of value, their skills being limited to the manipulation of investment instruments like "derivatives," which even they cannot fully explain—lost over *twelve trillion dollars* of other people's money thanks to the shady practices that tanked the stock market during that time. That's roughly 20 percent of the accumulated wealth of the United States, which it took a couple of centuries to build up, but less than two years to obliterate. If that money were placed end to end in $1 bills, it would stretch to the sun and back to Earth *two times over*. This, the handiwork of that very group—rich, white, and mostly male—that we are told are superior in work ethic, insight and abilities relative to the black and brown, and to women of all colors. So no, the racial wealth gaps we see in this society surely can't be due to merit.

And yes, I know that some might think it untoward to make reference to the race of those who squandered all this wealth by their illegal, unethical or incompetent machinations; isn't their racial identity an irrelevant detail? Fair enough. Yet I think we know—whether or not we are prepared to acknowledge it—that if those criminal, unethical and incompetent hedge fund managers, derivatives traders and stock manipulators had been black or brown, we would surely have heard about their race, and little else. We would have been treated to one chorus after another of white resentment, voices asserting that those folks of color shouldn't have even been in those positions, and probably only got them because of affirmative action, rather than the merit system (better known as Daddy's personal contact list), which had historically procured the same jobs for the white frat boys who just tanked the economy.

And given the ubiquity of certain stereotypes concerning African Americans and criminality, had the Wall Street con men been black, there is little doubt that part of the narrative would have also concerned how their actions further "proved" the connection between race and predatory behavior. One can only wonder how such stereotypes manage to persist when one examines the blinding whiteness of the financial fraud at the root of the current economic crisis, and how it dwarfs the level of criminality to which folks of color occasionally stoop. The FBI estimates that the annual value of all property stolen in the nation (as of 2008) was around $6.1 billion. Even if *all* regular thefts in the United States were committed by blacks (and of course they aren't, by a long shot), this would still represent only about one-twentieth of one percent of the amount of wealth destroyed by the almost entirely white Wall Street claque of financial fraudsters. To put this in perspective, the amount of money wiped out by the misdeeds of the banksters is so large, it would be like street criminals stealing what they now steal in a year *every five hours, every day for a year.* And yet we are still more likely to fear a black or brown male crossing the street in our direction than we are to fear white stockbrokers, hedge fund managers or financial advisors, which tells us quite a lot about the persistence of racial bias and its effect on our judgment. So yes, race matters, if for no other reason than to make a point about how *some* folks' misdeeds get racialized, while those of others do not.

Race also matters in terms of the existing opportunity structure in the larger job market, far beyond the confines of Wall Street. According to a study that examined more than 100,000 businesses across the country, as many as 1.2 million instances of overt job discrimination occur annually against blacks, Latinos and Asian Americans, affecting as many as one-third of all job searches by persons of color in the United States each year. Additional research tells us that lighter-skinned immigrants, mostly from European nations, earn around 15 percent more than darker-skinned immigrants, even when all their respective qualifications and markers of personal productivity are the same. And according to the most recent annual data from 2009, even when a black person has a college degree, he or she is nearly twice as likely as one of us with a degree to be unemployed, while Latinos and Asian Americans with degrees are 40 percent more likely than we are to be out of work, with the same qualifications. Furthermore, even when comparing only persons working in management, business and finance jobs, those of us in such occupations typically earn about 30 percent more in weekly income than our counterparts of color, amounting to nearly $13,000 in additional earnings each year relative to African Americans and Latinos. Although these gaps don't necessarily indicate overt discrimination—they could very well suggest that whites are simply privy to more lucrative job networks due to informal connections—the results are the same: whites continue to enjoy advantages, and opportunities remain unequal for persons of color, no matter their qualifications.

Overall, the median income for white men who are between twenty-five and thirty-four years old (early in their careers) is one-third higher than the median for black men who are fifty-five to sixty-four years old and already nearing retirement. Research has even found that a white man with a criminal record is more likely to be called back for a job interview than a black man without one, even when their credentials are the same. So much for all that reverse discrimination we keep talking about.

Numerous studies also point to the ongoing problem of unequal housing opportunity and suggest that there are millions of cases of race-based housing discrimination occurring each year. One recent study found that when blacks have better credit, higher incomes, more reserve savings and less debt than we do, they are subjected to higher interest rates and generally treated worse by lenders in six out of ten instances. Even when credit backgrounds, income and other factors that can affect the terms of mortgage loans are the same for whites and persons of color, it is persons of color who are more likely to be steered to high-cost loan instruments with more onerous interest rates. Indeed, one study from just a few years back found that even high-income African Americans were more likely than low-income whites to end up with a high-cost subprime loan, and up to half of the subprime loans were given to people who should have qualified for lower rates (and mostly would have, had they been white). Largely because of unequal housing opportunity, even high-income persons of color are more likely than moderate-income whites to live in communities with high concentrations of poverty, which affects everything from access to word-of-mouth job networks to the schools that children of such families will attend.

And speaking of schools, in the realm of education, racial disparities continue unabated as well. According to a recent comprehensive report from the Department of Education, schools that serve mostly African American students have twice as many teachers with only a year or two of experience as schools that serve white students, even when those schools are in the same districts. Also, new teachers in majority-minority schools are *five times* as likely as new teachers in mostly white schools to be uncertified in the subject matter they are currently being asked to teach.

Research has even found that within given schools, the least experienced and least effective teachers are regularly matched with the most challenging students in terms of prior academic performance (who are often low-income students of color in need of highly capable instruction), while the most experienced and effective teachers are paired with white, high-achieving students. Such results often stem from decisions made by white principals or from pressure exerted by white parents to get the "best" teachers for their children. Given the long-standing evidence that teachers with the most experience and highest levels of certification have the best track records for student achievement, the racial implications of this kind of inequity should be obvious. Indeed, the matching of inexperienced and ineffective educators with students of color and low-income students, combined with the pairing of more experienced and effective teachers with white students, perpetuates racial achievement gaps and contributes to larger societal inequity.

Further exacerbating racial disparity in education, those schools that serve mostly black and Latino students are also more than ten times as likely as the schools most of our kids attend to be places of concentrated poverty, and they are far less likely to offer a full complement of advanced classes. And, of course, schools with mostly white students typically receive more money per pupil for direct instruction than schools serving mostly students of color. Then, in what amounts to a cruel joke, after having provided unequal and unstandardized educational resources—from funding to teacher quality to curriculum offerings—our schools administer *standardized* tests, which are used to determine everything from whether students will be allowed to receive a diploma to whether schools themselves will be allowed to continue operating to where students will be able to go to college (if at all).

Although many of us have long argued that money isn't really what makes a difference in schools—and therefore, inequities in resources aren't really the problem—we must also acknowledge that none of us are clamoring to switch places or to have our kids switch places with the students of color who attend less well-funded institutions, hoping to make up for the difference with good values and a solid work ethic. As is so often the case, those who say money doesn't matter typically have money, so to them, it doesn't matter.

More evidence of modern-day racial bias manifests in the criminal justice system. Back in 1964, about two-thirds of all those incarcerated in this country were white, while one-third were persons of color. By the mid-1990s, those numbers had reversed, so that now, two-thirds of persons locked up are black and brown, while only a third are white. This shift was not the result of a change in who commits crime—the relative rates of criminal offending didn't change significantly in the intervening years—but rather stemmed mostly from the disproportionate concentration of justice system resources in communities of color, especially due to the so-called War on Drugs. Although whites comprise roughly 70 percent of all drug users and are every bit as likely as people of color to use drugs (contrary to popular perception), nine in ten people locked up each year for a possession offense are people of color. Black youth are nearly *fifty times* as likely as our youth to be incarcerated for a first-time drug offense, even when all the factors surrounding the crime (like whether or not a weapon was involved) are equal. Even though they are *less* likely than we are to be found with drugs or other illegal contraband when searched by police, blacks and Latinos are far *more* likely than we are to be stopped and searched by law enforcement looking for such items.

The incarceration spiral for persons of color then further contributes to an uneven opportunity structure in the larger society by depressing the likely earning potential of ex-offenders once they're released from jail or prison. Because of persistent biases against those with criminal records (especially persons of color with such records) and assumptions that they make for dishonest or unreliable employees, ex-offenders are far more likely than others to be unemployed, and they earn far less upon returning to the free world than others of comparable age, education and productivity.

So even in this, the so-called "age of Obama," evidence of institutional racial inequity and even outright institutional discrimination persists.

Most of us, I'm sure, are largely unaware of these facts, and in many ways that has always been the case. We have long been in denial about the reality of racism, even back in the day when, in retrospect, it was blatant. Even in the early 1960s, before the passage of civil rights legislation, most of us, according to Gallup polls, failed to see that the nation had a race problem. Even as African Americans were being hosed down and blown up in Birmingham, beaten in Selma, murdered in Mississippi and segregated and isolated up North, two-thirds of us said blacks had equal opportunity in employment, education and housing. In one 1962 survey, roughly 90 percent of us said that we believed black children had just as good a chance to get a quality education as we or our children did. That we may see such beliefs as borderline delusional now does not change the fact that we believed them to be quite rational at the time.

What does it say about us that even when the nation was characterized by official and quite legal white supremacy, we mostly failed to appreciate the obvious?

What it says to me is that our judgment on the matter is perhaps not the best. It says that perhaps we'd do well to listen to the voices of those who have been and continue to be targeted by racial discrimination, and not those who have had the option of ignoring it. *They* say we have a problem. And unless we wish to adopt the fundamentally racist view that we know their reality better than they know it—perhaps because they are "too emotional," or lack objectivity, or are too unintelligent to discern the contours of their own lived experiences—we should probably believe them. It isn't that we are incapable of seeing the truth. But having the luxury of remaining oblivious to the experiences of people of color (we aren't tested on it as a condition of obtaining academic or professional credentials, after all), we simply have little reason to know any better, whether in 1962 or today.

And yes, it's true, not *all* people of color agree about the extent to which racism remains a problem. I am well aware that there are black conservatives, about whom many of us seem quite animated, who insist that everything I am saying here is wrong; they believe, for instance, that there are no real barriers to opportunity any longer, and they hold themselves up as proof. But doesn't it seem problematic that we would so readily rely on the opinions of a statistical handful of the black community for our insights concerning that community? That we would so readily dismiss the expressed realities of the vast majority of persons of color, cleaving instead to the perspectives offered by those who not only constitute a small minority of those communities, but have minimal connections to those communities: people who work for white-led organizations and think tanks, live in white communities, and in some cases even brag about having left the black community behind?

If I were to suggest that the period during which blacks were enslaved hadn't really been that bad, and utilized as my evidence for such a position the testimony of those blacks (yes, they did exist) who, despite being deprived of personhood, swore that whites treated them well, would any rational person consider that testimony credible? Were someone to propose that the cruelty of white enslavers could be judged just as well, or even better, by those black folks who informed them of pending slave rebellions as by those who planned and carried out such rebellions—or that since most of the enslaved didn't run away, we should presume the business of trafficking and enslavement benign—who would proclaim such inanity reasonable? The answer, of course, is that while few would think such a thing reasonable now, most of our people thought exactly that during the period in question. Indeed, Dr. Samuel Cartwright, a well-respected physician of his day, insisted that only mental illness (what he called *drapetomania*) could cause enslaved black folks to run away from the plantation system within which they toiled. And whenever possible, white folks *did* proclaim the system of enslavement benign, by holding up the apparent "loyalty" of those they owned—since they mostly stayed put and very few went the way of Nat Turner—as proof. Even more, whites pointed to African Americans like Booker T. Washington, whose acceptance of segregation and second-class black citizenship—he eschewed agitation for voting rights or an end to racist laws in favor of black thrift and self-help—fit more neatly with our sensibilities.

No, I am not claiming a direct parallel between the current period and the period of slavery; the analogy is not between the system of oppression then and the ongoing problem of racism today. I am quite aware of the differences, as are, I assure you, people of color who insist that racism in the present is a real and persistent matter. The analogy is, instead, to the way so many of us have, in every generation, sought out the testimonials of utterly unrepresentative outliers within the nation's communities of color to ratify the system most of us already believed to be just and fair, never taking note of the irony involved: the implicit suggestion that black people really do understand their lives, but only when their understanding mirrors our own.

⚭

As for our understanding of these issues, which can be gleaned fairly easily by looking at recent survey data, it appears that a disproportionate number—certainly a clear majority—believe the following, in no particular order of importance:

First, that the real thing holding people of color back— especially black folks—is not racism, but rather their own behavioral pathologies, personal choices and dysfunctional cultural values, as manifested in high rates of out-of-wedlock childbirth, reliance on public assistance and general devaluation of educational achievement.

Second, that if people of color—and again, especially black folks—would simply try harder, they could make it. The problem, in other words, is that such persons lack the willpower to "pull themselves up out of poverty." Plenty of other groups (like the Irish, Italians and Jews) have pulled themselves up, and even Asians, a non-European group, have done so. If they can do it, anyone can, with sufficient effort.

Third, that even if racism remains a problem, dwelling on the matter or making too big an issue of it will only harm people of color, encouraging them to adopt a "victim mentality" and thereby sapping individual initiative. In other words, we shouldn't discuss racism too much, for the sake of the very people affected by it.

And *fourth*, that it is unfair to criticize the United States for racism in the past or present; after all, every nation has had its problems with discrimination and inequality. If anything, America has done more than these other places to make things right and to create an equal-opportunity society, and black and brown folks are better off here than anywhere else on earth: a point that ostensibly mitigates against continued discussion of racial injustice here.

Because these positions are so common, and at first glance may seem reasonable to many, I'll spend some time addressing them before moving on to more important issues. I understand, after all, where these types of perspectives come from, even if I view them to be largely without merit. Much of what we've been told over the years by parents, friends, the media—or politicians competing for our votes and using racially tinged imagery to obtain them—has made its mark and warped our thinking. It is hardly surprising that many of us, having been misled around a whole host of racial subjects, would have developed a mentality in which beliefs like those above would find a comfortable home.

The quite common position, that black social pathology and lack of effort explain the economic status of African Americans, rather than racism, confuses two related, yet somewhat distinct issues: racism and poverty. Even if I were to grant, for instance, that black poverty could be largely explained by internal dysfunctions within the black community (or what we sometimes like to refer to broadly as "black culture"), that would be irrelevant to the issue of racism facing people of color who are not poor. Even those black and brown folks who are well above the poverty line (and thus neither on public assistance nor often in single-parent homes) continue to struggle and face substantial disadvantages relative to their white counterparts.

As mentioned previously, even persons of color with college degrees, working in professional and managerial occupations, have far higher rates of unemployment and far lower wages than similar whites. Across virtually all job and educational attainment levels, blacks and Latinos with the same levels of education, working in the same occupations, routinely have double the rates of unemployment experienced by whites, and income-rich black and Latino households still have less than one-third the net worth as comparable whites, thanks to long-standing inherited advantages among our families. African American children from middle-class and affluent households are also far more likely than their white counterparts to attend high-poverty schools, to be relegated to low-track classes, and to be suspended or expelled from school altogether, despite breaking serious school rules no more often than white students from the same socioeconomic status. Middle-class and more affluent blacks are also disproportionately the targets of subprime mortgage loans, paying much higher rates of interest than comparable white borrowers, and are subjected, according to the available evidence, to racial profiling of all types. In other words, even if all the conservative critiques of the black and brown poor were accurate, the issue of racism as a unique and independent contributor to the status of the black community, relative to the white community, would remain.

But of course, the critiques of the black and brown poor are largely inaccurate, and the attempt to use such stereotypical imagery as a way to blame them for their own condition, and thereby skirt the issue of racism, is irresponsible in the extreme.

As for out-of-wedlock childbirth, many of us are quick to point out that rates of so-called "illegitimacy" have grown so substantially in the black community (now representing over 70 percent of all African American births) that we can hardly be surprised that most black children and families will be struggling economically. Although it is certainly true that single-parent homes typically have a harder time, financially, than two-parent homes, it is simply not the case that changes in the structure of the black family are to blame for racial disparities between whites and blacks. According to one study from the 1990s—at which point the out-of-wedlock birth rates in the black community had already climbed to their current high levels—even if these rates had remained the same since the 1960s and not budged upward at all, nearly all the income and poverty-rate gaps between whites and blacks would have remained the same. Even black married couples are twice as likely as their white counterparts to be poor, and Latino married couples are more than *four times* as likely as married whites to be poor. Currently, nearly one in five black children growing up in a two-parent home lives in poverty, more than double the rate for white children, while one in four Latino/a kids in a two-parent home remains poor—roughly equal to the rate at which white children in single-mother families experience poverty. And when black and Latina women are single moms, they are nearly twice as likely as our single moms to be poor. In other words, it is not single parenthood *per se* that explains the deprivation of persons of color relative to whites.

Indeed, much of the imagery of irresponsible

black women (especially teenagers) having babies they can't afford is itself irresponsible, in that it so wildly misleads those who are exposed to that imagery. The fact is, birth rates for black women under the age of eighteen (almost all of them unmarried) have fallen by more than a third since the early 1990s, and fertility rates among all unmarried black women have plummeted since the 1970s. The reason the share of black babies being born out of wedlock has increased, despite these two statistical trends, is that two-parent black couples are having far fewer children than similar couples in previous generations. If "intact" black families have far fewer children, those children who *are* born in the black community will show an increased ratio born "out of wedlock," but this will have little to do with irresponsible behavior on the part of single black folks, whose behavioral norms have only "improved" (using our apparent definition of that concept) in recent decades.

As for public assistance, the majority of people of color don't receive any; hence it is hardly legitimate to blame so-called "welfare" for the larger community's condition. Although people of color are more likely than whites to receive some form of income or health care assistance (which only makes sense, considering such groups are two to four times more likely to be poor) in any given month, fewer than four in one hundred blacks and fewer than three in one hundred Latinos receive cash welfare, between 6 and 12 percent receive some kind of housing assistance, and only 11 to 19 percent receive nutritional assistance (so-called "food stamps"). Considering that these recipients often overlap (particularly for cash and food assistance), the overall numbers of persons of color receiving benefits of these types is at no point greater than perhaps one in seven. Even then, benefits are paltry and hardly sufficient to encourage laziness or to serve as a serious disincentive to productive labor. Indeed, the median *monthly* value of cash and food assistance combined comes to only $255 per person—far lower in some states. Are we really to believe that any substantial number of persons would forgo a job so they could sit back and collect a few hundred dollars per month in benefits, leaving them still desperately impoverished?

Significantly, and contrary to common belief, most adults who receive cash assistance (the most vilified of all public assistance programs) are not able-bodied scam artists gaming the system and unwilling to work; rather, nearly eight in ten are either already working, looking regularly for work but unable to find a job, in school, or unable to work because of a persistent health condition. With jobs so hard to come by—even McDonald's recently held a massive national employee search, in which they were only able to hire six out of every hundred applicants—it is hardly fair to blame poor folks for their unemployment or occasional need to rely on public assistance. And the emphasis should indeed be on the word *occasional* here, as most persons who turn to one or another form of government help do not remain on the programs for long periods. For cash assistance, the typical recipient receives benefits for only five months; for food stamps, the typical duration for benefits is a little less than eight months; for housing assistance, the typical duration is only four months. Yet despite all this we continue to believe, at least most of us, that people of color are taking advantage of "welfare" and that this is what explains everything from their own economic condition to the nation's current budgetary woes.

As for the widespread notion that people of color—especially blacks—place too little emphasis on educational accomplishment, once again, stereotypes and racial prejudices buttress this belief far more than the facts do. To begin with, is it really logical to ascribe an insufficient drive for education to people who cared so much for learning that under enslavement they risked serious punishment just to learn how to read English? Are we really to believe that a people who created their own schools, including colleges and universities, when whites were shutting them out of educational opportunities, need to be lectured about the value of learning?

It seems more likely that we are merely looking at differential outcomes for African Americans in schools—differentials that are quite real—and, after the fact, blaming those differences on presumed gaps in values, rather than deeper structural conditions. Some of these were mentioned earlier: significant funding differentials between mostly white and mostly of-color schools; high concentrations of poverty in the latter as opposed to the former; different levels of teacher quality in mostly white as opposed to mostly of-color schools; and racial disparities in access to advanced curriculum.

In fact, research on the ways people from different races view schooling indicates that there is very little difference between racial and ethnic groups when it comes to how much their members value the importance of learning and doing well in school. Black youth are just as likely as white youth—sometimes even more likely—to say that doing well in school is important to them, their families and their friends. One study that looked at 40,000 students in grades seven through eleven actually found that it was white males—in other words, many of us and our children—who were the least likely of any group to say that good grades were "very important" to them. Another study, which examined measures of academic honesty and integrity among students in different racial and ethnic groups, found that it was we and our children who were more likely than kids of color to believe it was acceptable to cheat, cut class or talk back to teachers. In fact, the group that had the lowest measures of academic integrity were affluent whites—this was the most likely subgroup of all to endorse cheating and various corner-cutting techniques to get ahead without hard work. If anything, it is students of color who manifest better values when it comes to learning, but the opportunity structure continues to favor white students, resulting in unequal outcomes and the perpetuation of racial inequity. In short, we cannot blame different value systems, rooted in racial identity, for different educational outcomes between white students and students of color. Their values are largely the same. Their opportunities are anything but.

Looking at our second deflection of responsibility—the notion that all people of color need to do is deploy greater work effort and willpower in order to succeed—it is hard to imagine a more unjust and ultimately racist argument. To begin with, listen to that position, stated perhaps a bit more colloquially, but ultimately with the same underlying logic:

"Blacks aren't behind because of racism. They're behind because they're lazy."

I want everyone to really mull that one over—read it again, two or three times if need be, until the fundamental contradiction and racist irony of the statement itself are crystal clear. It's like one of those "magic eye" books our kids have, the ones where you blur your vision and suddenly hidden images appear that you hadn't seen before. Do you see it yet? In our denial of racism we are insisting that blacks as a group are defective. Yet that notion of group defect is the textbook definition of a racist belief, and if large numbers of us believe that argument to be true, how realistic is it to then presume we would be capable of responding in an unbiased and equitable manner when faced with a black job applicant, loan applicant or student in a classroom?

Beyond that, do we really believe that black folks need to be lectured about hard work, in a nation where, for generations, they were forced to do the *hardest* and most exacting labor in the entire country? In a nation where they provided as much as *$1 trillion* in unpaid labor under the system of enslavement? Do such a people as this truly need to be shown the value of work by those who benefited most from that unpaid labor: a group that includes millions of persons whose parents have, for generations, handed down opportunities, jobs and substantial fortunes to us, regardless of work effort?

Are we to believe that blacks would *choose* to remain three times as likely as whites to be poor, rather than work harder? That they *enjoy* the excess mortality that derives from their current status at the bottom of the nation's racial and class structure—currently 100,000 black folks die each year who wouldn't if their mortality rates were level with those of whites—and opt to continue down that road, rather than work harder to survive? Can differential work efforts and values really explain why African American households today have median incomes that are one-third lower, adjusted for inflation, than what white households were bringing in *forty years ago*? Are gaps such as these realistically the outgrowth of differential *willpower* alone? Along the same lines, do Latinos—so many of whom work in hot ✳ fields picking fruit, or clean up after us in hotels, and who generally work long hours at some of the most demanding jobs in the nation—need to be taught how to work hard by white people? Surely we can't be serious when we say these kinds of things.

Of course, there is no evidence that people of color have different work ethics than whites. On any measure of such work ethic—such as the number of hours put in on the job, amount of time spent looking for work when unemployed, willingness to work at a relatively low wage, and willingness to upgrade one's skills and retrain for a new job—there is either no racial difference between whites and persons of color, or the differences that exist *favor* those who are black and

Important

brown, suggesting an even *greater* desire on their parts to work and work hard. Currently, of persons who are twenty to sixty-four years old and not working, whites are three times as likely as similar African Americans to say that the reason they aren't working is because they are "not interested" in having a job; blacks who are not working are 2.5 times as likely to be out of work because they can't find work, despite looking consistently.

And really, now—using the history of the Irish, Italians or Jews as evidence that anyone can make it? To begin with, black folks, indigenous peoples and most Latinos—especially Mexican Americans—have always been constructed as outside the orbit of white civilization. Even though European ethnic groups faced discrimination, they were never the objects of caste-like oppression. They may have started out "provisional" members of the white club, but within a very short time were given permanent passes. In large part, white ethnic advance came as the direct *flip side* of black and brown marginalization. Indeed, working-class Europeans had rights and opportunities (like voting and land ownership) extended to them at the very moment free blacks were being stripped of those same rights (during the Jacksonian period); and later, large-scale immigration of Irish, Italians and Eastern European Jews swelled just when immigration from non-European nations was all but shut down. In many ways, these white ethnic groups were used as a buffer between the WASP elite and persons of color, often played off against them in an attempt to divide the loyalties of folks who were in similar class groupings.

Most European immigrants came to the North at a time when industry was the key to growth thus, they were well positioned to benefit from the opportunities afforded by the modern economy. Blacks, on the other hand, were relegated mostly to the agricultural South, which offered fewer opportunities for advancement. Upon migrating north in search of a better life for their families, African Americans encountered massive violence and race riots (often led by those white ethnics who wished to remain one step ahead of people of color), as well as labor union discrimination and residential segregation, in ways that even the most despised European ethnic did not.

Of course, there is that seemingly sticky matter of Asian success, some of us might reply. They aren't white, after all, and haven't been able to "become white" over time, yet they've done well. And looked at a certain way, it's true; the data seem to indicate widespread Asian American success and economic accomplishment. Indeed, as many of us are quick to point out, household income among Asian Americans is higher than that for whites, as are the rates at which Asian Americans have college or advanced degrees.

But before we get carried away with this seeming proof of racism's demise, let's step back a bit and consider a few things.

To begin, let's remember that a disproportionate percentage of Asian Americans came to the United States already having educational and occupational status that would place them in the middle class or above: large numbers, in fact, either already had a college degree or were working on their degree at the time of arrival here. This makes Asian Americans a highly self-selected immigrant group—quite different from, and hardly comparable to, either native-born African Americans, indigenous peoples or most Latinos, who came over a contiguous border with the United States.

Second, let us recall that Asian Americans are far from monolithic: some are doing pretty well, while others are struggling. Poverty rates, for instance, among Chinese Americans and Vietnamese Americans are 50 percent higher than the poverty rates for whites; Korean American poverty rates are two-thirds higher than the rates for whites; and poverty rates for Cambodian, Hmong and Lao Americans are *2.5 times* higher than white poverty rates.

What's more, those poverty rate differences between whites and Asians are nationwide aggregate figures; the real situation, in specific communities, is far worse. As it turns out, one of the principal reasons

Asian American household income, on the whole, is higher than white household income, is that Asian Americans are concentrated in a handful of places with disproportionately high incomes relative to the rest of the country—but also much higher *costs of living*. So, for instance, 55 percent of all Asian Americans live in just six places: Los Angeles, New York, San Francisco, Honolulu, Washington, D.C., and Chicago. For this reason their incomes will tend to be higher, and especially when compared to those of whites, who in the aggregate are not concentrated in such places. But when we compare only whites and Asian Americans living in the same communities, we find that Asian poverty rates are routinely double the rates for whites. In other words, despite their relatively high skills and oftentimes greater educational attainment relative to whites, Asian Americans are not doing nearly as well as comparable whites are.

Indeed, Asian Americans earn less than whites with the same educational attainment, whether we're comparing high school dropouts, those with diplomas or those with college degrees. As just one example, consider that Chinese Americans in professional occupations (who are a highly educated group) earn only 56 percent as much as their white counterparts. And the only reason that Asian household income tops that for whites, on average, is because Asian households tend to be larger and have more income earners per household than our households. Despite their much higher average educational attainment—thanks to the aforementioned selective immigration—per capita income remains lower for Asian Americans than for whites. So much for the model minority myth, and so much for the notion of equal opportunity.

But even when we know these things, and accept that racism and discrimination are real, some among us still try valiantly to avoid the conversation around such matters. In those instances, we insist that irrespective of the facts, it is best to downplay such problems because to speak of racial injustice and discrimination, especially in the present day, is to encourage a "victim mentality" among people of color. According to this argument, to discuss discrimination is to encourage black and brown folks to see themselves as perpetual targets of white racism.

Yet as commonly as this argument manifests within our community, if we examine it honestly, it stands out as extraordinarily presumptuous and even racist in many ways. The reason I suggest the argument is racist is that it seems to presume that persons of color are too stupid to already know what it is they're experiencing, or have experienced, historically. Those who bemoan the so-called victim mindset appear to believe that no one would think about racism were it not for the constant presence of liberals and leftists raising the issue. Second, the argument supposes that black and brown folks are so weak-willed that if they understood the obstacles in their way, they would crumble like cheap piecrust.

Yet, sadly, by an early age most folks of color are well aware of the negative stereotypes held about their racial groups. Indeed, recent evidence indicates an awareness of these stereotypes as early as the third grade, and rarely later than the fifth: around the age of, say, eleven. This awareness is not due to liberals bringing it up, but rather the result of black and brown folks *living* with the mistreatment that stems from the stereotypes and being exposed to them regularly. No, talking about racism isn't the problem: racism itself is. To blame the conversation for the problem is like blaming your speedometer for the speeding ticket you just received.

Naturally, none of us who worry about people of color adopting a debilitating mindset of victimhood ever fret about the same thing happening to others who have been victimized by injustice. We don't tell Jewish folks to get over the Holocaust, or not to talk about those unhappy matters, lest they cripple themselves under the weight of a victim syndrome. Keep in mind that there has been steady support for curricula that address the destruction of European Jewry under Hitler, and no one has suggested that teaching the *Diary of Anne Frank* might be debilitating to Jewish children. Likewise, we don't warn crime victims against the adoption of a victim mindset. No indeed, many of us even praise "victims' rights" groups, as if to suggest that, for these poor souls, victimhood is a status to be venerated and even utilized for the purpose of political influence. Thus we are regularly treated to representatives of "victims' rights" groups on news programs whenever crime policy is being discussed, as if the mere fact of having lost a loved one to violent crime somehow imbued one with special insights about the best public policies for making our communities safe. So why is it acceptable for these other groups' members to focus on their victimization, while it's somehow untoward or even self-destructive for people of color to do so?

To discuss racism and discrimination is to prepare for its possibility, even while one works hard to overcome its sting. There is no logic whatsoever to the belief that having been forewarned, one must by necessity shrivel up in fear, or slack off, convinced that one hasn't a chance to succeed. Indeed, the whole history of black America makes that case convincingly. After all, if you were to ask most any black Americans over the age of forty what their parents told them about race when they were younger, what you would hear in reply is as straightforward as it is virtually unanimous: that they would have to work twice as hard as white folks. And why was this so? Precisely *because* the system was so profoundly unjust and discrimination so deeply ingrained that, despite their best efforts and talent, they would too often be overlooked for the best jobs and opportunities solely because of the color of their skin.

But does anyone condemn the older African Americans who previously prepared generations of blacks for hard work and success by telling them in no uncertain terms that things were unequal and unfair? Do we believe that blacks in prior eras were crippling their children with the message that they would need to work harder than whites because of racism? Better still, is there any evidence whatsoever that being told such a thing did in fact injure black folks, or make them try less hard than they otherwise might have? If anything, the exact opposite is true. Knowing the odds, black and brown folk tried even *harder*, because to do otherwise would have all but guaranteed defeat. In short, the claim that discussing racism and discrimination turns people of color into passive victims flies in the face of every bit of empirical evidence on the subject. Knowing the truth inspires perseverance and passionate *resistance* to victimization, not resignation to one's status as a target.

With all this said, however, there is that one final

default position to which we so quickly retreat when confronted with the evidence of this nation's racist past and present. It's the one about how the United States, however flawed, is really no different from any other country when it comes to such a history. The whole of human existence, after all, has involved a process of certain groups oppressing others. And haven't we in the United States done more to address and rectify that history than most? Aren't black and brown folks far better off here than they would be virtually anywhere else on Earth?

Putting aside whether or not any of those suggestions is true, every one of them is irrelevant. Injustice in one place cannot be dismissed or rendered unworthy of rectification just because there is another injustice of equal or even greater magnitude happening elsewhere. So, for example, one could not argue that Holocaust survivors have nothing to complain about, since after all, they could have been one of the many millions slaughtered by Stalin. To argue that one injustice cancels out the moral claim of victims of other injustices makes no sense, and does intellectual violence to the very notion of rational thought.

Extending this logic to its ultimate conclusion would lead to some especially appalling positions. Among them, one could say that even under Jim Crow segregation, African Americans probably had it better than, say, black folks in the Belgian Congo—where millions were being slaughtered and worked to death by King Leopold—and therefore, instead of trying to end apartheid here, black folks should have just sucked it up and thanked the Lord for their good fortune. Indeed, following the trajectory of this mindset, one could argue that the United States could even reinstate segregation, and so long as the system remained somewhat less vicious than conditions in some other society, there would be no great injustice in doing so, or at least none worth protesting.

In short, this is the logic of passing the buck, tantamount to what so many of us did as kids, when, having broken a window playing ball—and having been caught in the act by our mothers—we protested that Billy was also throwing the ball, so it wasn't only our fault. As I recall (and I doubt any of your experiences are that different), Mom didn't much care about Billy. If memory serves, she asked something about whether, if Billy decided to throw himself from a bridge, we would, in the manner of a damned fool, follow his example. In other words, we have to take responsibility for our piece of the problem, even though, to be sure, there are others in need of the same self-examination.

The bottom line is that regardless of whatever progress we have made on these matters—and of course we've made quite a bit in certain areas—and however much things may be objectively worse elsewhere, like must be compared with like. Americans of color are *Americans*, after all, and so their measure of opportunity must be viewed relative to other Americans, not in relation to those in Rwanda or Bosnia or North Korea or anywhere else on earth. To tell them to stop complaining about racism because things could be worse elsewhere is no more appropriate than it would have been to tell the Irish upon arrival in the United States to stop worrying about the discrimination they faced here, since, after all, they could still be starving back home. Along these same lines, I suspect that many of us who point to other nations when the issue of racism here is broached would not like it much were someone to suggest that we should stop complaining about taxes, since, if we lived in pretty much any other industrialized nation on earth, those taxes would be much higher. So ya' know, maybe we should shut up already and stop whining.

∞

Look, I know that many of us thought that by now we'd be done with all this chatter about the problem of race in America. Right after the election of Barack Obama, I started getting tons of emails saying one or another version of that very point: the election of a man of color proved once and for all that racism was no longer a real issue in this country. How *could* it be, if such a man could win the presidency?

Well, far be it from me to ignore the election of a black man as president, or suggest that such a thing was meaningless. Of course it means something. Obviously, were this nation the same place it was fifty or even twenty years ago, that electoral outcome would have been unthinkable. But before we take even as significant a development as this to signal a sea change in white racial attitudes—the putting away of a racist past for the warm embrace of a multicultural future—we might do well to remember a few things, not the least of which is that most whites, even in many relatively "liberal" blue states, voted *against* Barack Obama in that election. Now, I'm not saying that voting against Obama makes one a racist, but if we're going to use his victory as proof that racism is dead, we at least have to remember that he only won because of the votes of people of color and *young* whites, while losing by landslide proportions in every other white demographic. Indeed, whites were generally so unenthused by his candidacy that overall white turnout at the polls in 2008 was down by over 700,000 voters.

But even more instructive has been the upsurge in white anger aimed at this president, which has so often manifested in blatantly racist ways.

For instance, we've repeatedly witnessed white

conservative activists coming to rallies with signs picturing the president as an African witch doctor with a bone through his nose, or sending around emails picturing the White House lawn covered with watermelons, or portraying the first family as chimpanzees or some such thing. Likewise, the Republican candidate for governor of New York in 2010—a favorite of the conservative right—sent an email to his friends, for which he refused to apologize, in which the president was portrayed in a pimp costume and a picture of traditional Zulu dancers was referred to as an "Obama inauguration rehearsal."

Only slightly less blatant are the ways right-wing commentators have stoked the fires of white anxiety by portraying the president as somehow being out to get us. To wit, the claim that President Obama's health care reform legislation is really just a backdoor way to obtain reparations for slavery on behalf of black Americans, an argument forwarded by wildly influential media personality Glenn Beck—wildly influential because millions of us made him so. Along the same bizarre and yet politically astute line, consider Rush Limbaugh, who has claimed that the president is deliberately trying to destroy the economy and is "happily" presiding "over the decline of America" as "payback" for the history of racism and slavery. Though these kinds of arguments are absurd on their face (what kind of reparations, after all, require one to get sick first, in order to get paid?), they are effective tools for whipping up anxiety and anger in a time of social change and insecurity.

Or consider Eric Bolling of Fox Business News, who recently accused the president of hosting "hoodlums in the hizzouse"—using hip-hop slang to characterize the first family's home—all because Obama had met with the leader of Gabon in the White House and had invited rapper Common (whose lyrics are anything *but* gangsterish) to a presidential event a few weeks earlier. This was close on the heels of Bolling's prior remarks that Obama should stop "chugging forties" in Ireland—a reference to forty-ounce bottles of malt liquor stereotypically associated with African Americans—and come home to check out the devastation wrought by tornadoes in Missouri. Though the president had indeed been photographed having a pint of beer in an Irish pub, it most certainly had not been a "forty," as Bolling had to have known. The use of the imagery was deliberate, a dog whistle to those of us who still can't quite deal with the presence of a black man atop the nation's political system.

So too, Donald Trump's recent critique of the president, which, rather than focusing on his policies, took aim at his academic credentials. Despite Barack Obama having graduated *magna cum laude* from Harvard Law,

Trump floated the idea (shortly before deciding not to run for president himself) that perhaps Obama hadn't deserved to get into the Ivy League schools from which he'd graduated with honors. Indeed, Trump noted, he had many friends with kids who'd been turned down from those institutions despite "fantastic" test scores. This slam on the president—essentially a way of characterizing him as just another affirmative action beneficiary who probably only got into good schools because of race, thereby bumping some white kid from a slot they deserved—was nothing if not transparent. And coming from a man who had openly and proudly supported the McCain-Palin ticket—whose members, respectively, graduated fifth from the bottom of their class and attended five schools in six years, barely graduating at all—it reeked of hypocrisy and racial resentment.

None of these attacks by leading members of the conservative cognitariat have been accidental or incidental; neither are they the only examples of blatant appeals to white racial resentment and anxiety that have been seen in recent years. They are, however, a good indication that we are far from the post-racial moment that so many saw fit to proclaim after the election of the nation's first president of color. Just as sexism failed to disappear in India, Pakistan, Great Britain or Israel following the election of women as heads of state in those places, so too, racism remains a reality in the United States, irrespective of the color of the nation's president.

And for those of us who consider ourselves liberal, left or progressive—and perhaps voted for President Obama—we can't be smug either. The truth is, a poll taken just a month before the election in 2008 found that a large percentage of white Democrats who intended to vote for Obama nonetheless admitted to holding any number of racist stereotypes about blacks to be true. So the fact that many were willing to carve out an exception for this one black guy, while still viewing the larger black community negatively, hardly acquits us of the charge that we too may have some stuff to work on. Research on subconscious and implicit racial bias has found the vast majority of us, myself included, have internalized certain racist and prejudicial beliefs about people of color. Not because we are bad people, let alone bigots, or even because we are "racists" at our core, but simply because we are *here*, and advertising works, and we've been subjected to a lot of negative advertising, so to speak, when it comes to those who are not white in this society.

For instance, news coverage of crime overrepresents people of color as criminal offenders, relative to the percentage of crime such persons actually commit, thereby contributing to widespread stereotypes about black and brown criminality. As a result of years of conditioning, research has found, when whites are hooked up to brain-scan imaging machines and exposed to even subliminal images of black men, flashed on a screen for mere milliseconds, roughly nine in ten show dramatically increased activity in the part of the brain that is activated when a person is afraid. The fact that we are four to five times more likely to be criminally victimized by another white person than by a black person doesn't appear to change our assumptions about who poses the greatest risk to our safety and well-being.

Other research shows that we are far more likely to perceive aggression and violence in a person of color than in a white person, even when both exhibit similar behaviors. So, for instance, in one classic study, groups of whites were shown a video in which two men—one black and one white—were arguing. When the white man (who was an actor) shoved the black man at the end of the argument, only 17 percent of whites viewing the incident said they perceived the act as violent; but when the black actor administered the shove, three of four whites said they perceived the act as a violent one.

In fact, sadly, even people of color sometimes internalize negative views about themselves. A recent study—mirroring similar research from more than a half century ago—found that African American children tend to prefer white dolls to black dolls, because they view the former as "good" and "nice" while they see the latter as "mean" and "stupid."

In many ways it's not surprising that we would all be susceptible to internalizing these types of racial biases. Even without any direct instruction or conditioning, adopting views that are racially prejudicial comes easily in a nation such as ours. If we grow up in a culture where we are told that everyone can make it if they try, and yet we can see that many have *not* "made it," and that certain groups are far worse off than others, it becomes almost logical to conclude that there must be something defective about those groups and something *better* about the groups at the top of the ladder. In other words, the combination of subjective ideology (the myth of meritocracy) and objective inequity (race-based stratification) creates the perfect recipe for the adoption of racist views as well as class bias. That so many of us would fall into that kind of cognitive trap hardly makes us bad people, let alone bigots. But it does mean we have issues. And it also means that unless we address these issues, the problems of institutional inequity will continue to fester.

And yes, I know it's not easy to hear any of this right now. Millions of us are hurting as well. As the economy has imploded in recent years, we too have been caught up in the maelstrom of financial insecurity: long-term unemployment, lack of adequate health care, foreclosed houses or mortgages we struggle to pay on time, or an inability to afford our kids' college education. I get it, I really do. Even if we sympathize with those persons of color who continue to face unequal opportunities and discrimination—be it overt or subtle—so long as we're facing serious economic setbacks and uncertainty ourselves, many among us may not feel like focusing on such matters. But we must, because the inequities faced by people of color, and the way we have long disregarded those inequities or assumed they weren't our problem, have led us directly to this current moment. In other words, our pain and their pain are connected, far more so than many of us may believe. Only by addressing the one can we ever hope to address the other.

To understand why this is so, we'll need to closely examine this particular moment and how we got here. Specifically, we'll need to interrogate some of the things that we as whites have long been able to take for granted, how those normative assumptions are being challenged at present, and how those challenges, and the social changes they portend, have intensified our insecurity, our fear and our anxiety about the future. In large part, the crisis of the current moment is only partially a material one; it is only partly about economic insecurity. More than that, it is about how a people can be set up by their own myths, their own internal narrative of their society—the story they tell themselves and others—in such a way as to leave them (us) ill-prepared for a changing and dynamic social reality. That is where we find ourselves today. It is at once a dangerous and yet portentous place to be.

∽

The fact is, things *are* changing in America, and in many ways we haven't been prepared for those changes. To be white has been to take a lot for granted over the years, and to assume that *our* normal was everyone's normal; that our way of seeing the country and the culture—and that our experiences within both—were the ones that mattered, and were normative for all. We could take for granted that the political leaders would look like us, as would the cultural icons: they would all have salt-of-the-earth biographies and chiseled jaws and wear cowboy hats like John Wayne, or for that matter, Ronald Reagan riding horseback on his ranch. They would all be Christians. We could take for granted that our communities would be filled mostly with people who looked like us, and whose cultural and religious traditions were similar to our own. We would not have to see or think about people of color too often, let alone rub shoulders with them daily, on the job or in the supermarket. We wouldn't see signs printed in languages other than English. We wouldn't even have "ethnic food" sections in our groceries. And a lot of us rather preferred it that way. Above all, we could take for granted a certain level of economic security, and rest assured that our narrative about the country—what makes us great and what we stand for—would be a narrative over which we would have ultimate control.

As harsh as it may sound to some of us, Toni Morrison had it right when she suggested, "In this country American means white. Everybody else has to hyphenate." When it came to understanding and envisioning the ideal American, to be white long meant to be the prototype, the floor model, of that national species. True enough, there were hundreds of indigenous nations within the borders of what we now call North America, long before the arrival of the first Europeans. So too, the Spanish brought and then abandoned a group of Africans off the coast of what is now South Carolina in the late 1500s, several decades before the Jamestown colony and even further in advance of the Mayflower. So yes, one could make the argument that there are persons of color who were and are more "American" than the Anglo colonists who, in the early seventeenth century, began the process of conquest, believing as they did in their God-given right to lay claim to lands beyond their shores.

One could make that argument, could have been

making it indeed for hundreds of years, but to what effect? No matter who was here first, whiteness and American identity have been joined at the hip for centuries; the sons and daughters of England, Ireland, Germany, Scotland and the like, have long been able to look in the mirror and see ourselves as the living embodiment of the American ideal. No matter their prior presence on these shores, the black, brown and red have forever and always had to lobby, petition, plead, scrape, fight and even die for the right to lay claim to that ideal as their own. They have been as perpetual outsiders, standing at the gates looking in, never as fully American as the lighter-skinned who resided within the walls of the national mansion and who—if not always immediately, certainly within a generation or so—were accepted as part of the family, jumping those who had been in line long before them.

Even the oft-heard and generally liberal cry that we are a "nation of immigrants" has presupposed that European identity and American identity were one. After all, indigenous people did not enter the country via Ellis Island, and neither did people of African descent. They were not immigrants except under the most tortured definition of that term. And so, in the classic *Schoolhouse Rock* cartoon "The Great American Melting Pot" we get the line: "America was the new world and Europe was the old," delivered merrily and without the slightest misgiving. America's melting pot concept was always conceived as a way to take people from various backgrounds and melt them into a new unitary whole, with the European taste predominating among the ingredients.

But now, white normativity is being challenged, and not only on one front, but on four: political, economic, cultural, and demographic. And each of these, in turn and especially together, poses a direct challenge to whiteness on yet a fifth front, the narrative front, by which I mean that battlefield of ideas within which the national character and story itself are defined and told to others.

First among the recent challenges to white normativity is the election of a black man to the very pinnacle of power: president and commander in chief of the United States of America. Although this may not seem a big deal to some—especially those who are younger and lack the historical context to understand the magnitude of such a thing—rest assured, there are millions for whom it is a very big deal indeed. Having grown up in a society where the leaders *all* looked like us, and had names like ours, and biographies similar to ours, to now have the nation led by someone whose father was *African*—not even African American, but *African*—and whose name is *Barack Hussein Obama*, and who lived *outside* the United States for a few of his earlier years, is to have our notions of political Americanness fundamentally challenged.

This is why during the run-up to the election, one could see T-shirts displaying the question: "If Obama wins, will they still call it the White House?" It's why so many white folks could be seen on YouTube expressing openly their fears about a black president, wondering whether he would enslave white people or in some way try to exact payback for centuries of racial inequity, or questioning his citizenship or his religion in ways never attempted for white candidates. Birtherism—the school of thought that holds Barack Obama to be something other than American—is inherently about the attempt to "other" those whose backgrounds are different from the so-called national norm. It is a way of saying he is *not* one of us, no matter the documentation provided, no matter the mountains of evidence that attest to his citizenship.

Then of course there is the economic insecurity that has caught us so off-guard. Double-digit unemployment, housing foreclosures, unaffordable health care, failing schools: none of this is new for those who are black or brown, but for us it is horrifyingly unique. It has been roughly three-quarters-of-a-century—three full generations dating back to the Great Depression—since we have collectively faced that kind of financial trauma and anxiety. Although some among us have known hardship and deprivation, to be sure (and I count myself in that number), as a group, as a collective body, white America has not seen this level of uncertainty in a very long time, well past the memories of most of us still alive. So that too proves unsettling and keeps us up at night. Even when we've faced periods of hardship before, we always had the faith that things would get better, and relatively soon, that this too would pass, and that our children would certainly do better than we had.

People of color had never been able to take any of this for granted, but we could, and that confidence buoyed us, even in our roughest days. But now, that faith has been shaken. Our assumptions about the opportunity structure have been thrown off balance, and having been so ill-prepared for such a thing, we find ourselves suffering not only the material insecurity that comes from a faltering economy, but also the psychological trauma borne of realizing that everything so many of us assumed about our country and the system under which we live may well have been wrong.

The economic insecurity we are now facing, for the first time in a long time, poses a challenge to one of the most cherished elements of the American narrative; namely, that the nation is a land of opportunity and meritocracy, where hard work and initiative allow even the lowliest individual to rise in the ranks, to go from rags to riches, and to make a way for themselves and their families. The notion that rugged individualism is all that is needed to "make it" has little credence in a society where millions—including millions who had long had the ultimate faith in its veracity—find themselves struggling no matter their effort.

What most of us never realized, but persons of color have always known, is that the U.S. economy is far more similar to a game of "Chutes and Ladders" than "Monopoly." It has long been a place where one's personal strategy for success and wealth building mattered far less than circumstance, or even the lucky or unlucky roll of the proverbial dice. One could begin to move up, climbing the ladder of intergenerational advance, only to land on a downward slide that could and often did send you or your children back to the metaphorical beginning. For us, the game was always upward and onward—ladders without chutes—but for everyone else, the chutes predominated and were to be found around every turn. Coming to terms with the reality—a reality about which persons of color have long been aware—can't be easy.

But in addition to the political and economic challenges to white normativity, there is more. A third concern is the rather dramatic cultural transformation of modern American society. Just a few decades ago most all the popular culture icons—in film, television, music and the like—were white like us. Even MTV, during its first several years on the air, refused to play any videos by black artists, with Michael Jackson being the first (and for a while the only) exception to a generally white rule. The cultural images beamed not only around the nation but also around the world were of a white America. But now, it is fair to say that American culture is thoroughly multicultural, with each thread of that cultural garment being intrinsically interlaced with the others. From the foods we eat to the music we hear to the clothing styles, there is no way to separate the various cultural and ethnic threads any longer. Hiphop has become the dominant popular cultural form in the United States, and comprises a significant part of the soundtrack of most young people's lives, including most young whites. We've got rap artists making records with country artists, and that Hootie guy is now one of the fastest rising stars in Nashville. Even small towns now have Indian and Vietnamese restaurants, authentic Mexican food and bodegas. And let's not forget the transformation of the religious landscape, in which we can see the addition of mosques and Hindu temples in communities that once held only churches and the occasional synagogue.

Finally, and perhaps most important, there is that rapidly changing demographic landscape that we keep hearing about in the media, or about which we ourselves whisper in hushed and occasionally nervous tones. According to projections, by no later than 2050, we will cease to be the majority in the Unites States. By then, we will have dipped to just under half of all Americans, while people of color will comprise the collective majority. In several states, this population shift has already happened, with whites comprising half or less of the population.

For a people who have been able to take our fundamental Americanness for granted, to suddenly be faced with the realization that we will have to share that designation with people who look different and pray differently and whose primary language may be different from our own, can be quite jarring for some of us. The club is no longer exclusive. The membership rolls are being opened up. In the process, the sense of "specialness" that American identity once held for us is being bid downward by the inclusion of some within its ranks who never would have qualified in decades and eras past. Within perhaps a decade or two, it may no longer be automatic that we envision a white person from the so-called "heartland" when the terms "all-American boy" or "all-American girl" are used; rather, we might envision a first-generation Latina immigrant in the Southwest, a Hmong farmer in Wisconsin, or an Arab Muslim in Dearborn, Michigan. How does that feel? Be honest.

Any one of these transformations on its own would be difficult for many of us to swallow, but together they create something of a perfect storm for white anxiety. And each of them poses a direct challenge to the national narrative, to the understanding of who we are and who we will be in years to come. These various blows to white normativity have made race salient for us for the first time. The old saying that "being white means never having to think about it," while perhaps true for most of our history, is becoming less and less true with each passing year. We *are* beginning to think about it. As the nation and our own communities become less white, as the popular culture becomes more multicultural, as the economy melts down, and as political leadership is exercised by a man of color with a name that seems strange and exotic to many of us, whiteness suddenly becomes highly visible. It becomes marked space: now we are *different* from the president; we are *different* from the celebrities on the posters in our kids' rooms; we are *different* from a lot of the people we see at the mall, or in the schools, or in our neighborhoods, and we are, surprisingly, *not that different* from millions of people of color when it comes to economic insecurity and hardship.

For centuries we have defined our status by way of our distance from the racial other. The closer we were to the black and brown, the less status we enjoyed. So a good neighborhood meant a white neighborhood, a good school meant a white school—those were the underlying assumptions of white flight, which began as soon as communities and schools came to have even small numbers of people of color in them. The custom of defining our status by the distance we were able to put between ourselves and racial others is the reason labor unions kept blacks and other people of color out of their ranks for so long. To integrate the workforce would be to diminish what W.E.B. DuBois called the "psychological wage of whiteness," by which he meant the kind of benefit one receives from being able to say that while you may not have much, at least you aren't black.

And so, as the social, cultural, political and perceived economic distance between us and *them* shrinks, it is predictable that such developments might come as a shock to our sense of all that is right and good; that such developments might make us anxious about the future and what it holds for us. A recent survey actually found, for instance, that despite the much worse conditions facing black America relative to white America—black folks are still far more likely to be out of work, poor, or in bad health, among other markers of social inequality—black people are far more optimistic about the future than we are. Whites, despite our ongoing advantages relative to the black and brown, are the most pessimistic of all racial groups in the nation. How do we make sense of such a thing? Clearly it cannot be because of objective evidence suggesting that we are the ones in the worst shape, because we are not, by any rational calculus. But we are the group that is having the hardest time adjusting to change, and that, one supposes, is what makes the difference.

In a strange way, it has been the very advantage and privilege that we have enjoyed relative to persons of color that has left us ill-equipped to deal with the setbacks of the current moment. With our expectations ever high, our sense that we were in control of our own destinies always secure, we could not conceive of the kind of downturn that so many of our number are now facing. Perhaps that's why *Newsweek* could run a cover story in spring 2011 concerning "beached white males," and how even white-collar white men were having trouble (so now, it was *really* a crisis!), and how so many of these former members of the corporate elite were completely unable to cope with the financial uncertainty to which they were, for the first time, being exposed.

Likewise, as the distance between us and people of color narrows, some appear to believe that whatever gains the black and brown have made in recent years—in terms of jobs or higher education access—have come directly at our expense. If *they* are making progress, it must be because *we* are being oppressed, discriminated against, or held back in some way. One recent Harvard study of our opinions about racism in America discovered that most of us actually think (despite the voluminous data to the contrary) that discrimination against *us* is more common than discrimination against people of color.

Having traveled across the country over the past sixteen years, and having spoken on hundreds of college and university campuses, I have often heard many fellow white Americans lament the existence of "minority scholarships" for which only students of color qualify. For many of us, such support amounts to a horrific and racist injustice against our people. Where are the white scholarships, some ask? What about *us*? And yet, to say these kinds of things requires a profound unwillingness to look at the bigger picture. After all, how can one view the rather minimal monies afforded by so-called minority scholarships as the racial injustice in the educational system, when we continue to have such embedded, institutionalized advantages from kindergarten on, as referenced previously?

More to the point, please keep in mind that according to a national study by the General Accounting Office, less than 4 percent of scholarship money in the United States is represented by awards that consider race as a factor at all, and only 0.25 percent (one-quarter of one percent) of all undergrad scholarship dollars come from awards that are restricted to persons of color alone. In other words, we are fully capable of competing for and receiving the other 99.75 percent of scholarship funds out there for college. Not to mention the fact that very few students of color actually receive these kinds of scholarships, with only 3.5 percent of all black and brown collegians receiving any award even *partly* based on race. So while we may *think* the people of color on our campus or our kids' campus are all the wards of some race-based preference scheme, the evidence suggests that at least 96.5 percent of them received no race-based scholarship funds at all.

Facts aside though, I can understand why so many of us might be afraid. As we become anxious, uncertain as to our future and where the nation is headed, that anxiety is being fed around every corner by right-wing commentators bent on using that uncertainty to fuel a political movement. The sad truth is, racial resentments are potent motivators in a nation such as ours, and there is no shortage of mouthpieces prepared to use them to their own ends, a subject to which I now turn.

∞

Consider the perverse logic of Rush Limbaugh's suggestion that President Obama was deliberately trying to destroy the American economy as some form of "pay-back" for slavery and racism, or Glenn Beck's charge that health care reform is really just Barack Obama's way to obtain reparations for slavery. Both allegations seem the stuff of absurdist and paranoid fantasy, and yet, in an era of white racial anxiety and resentment, they *couldn't be more rational.* They serve, almost perfectly, as triggers for our racial angers and insecurities. That black guy is trying to harm us, to take our money and give it to *them*, to make us hurt the way his people were hurt. Obama "hates white people," as Glenn Beck infamously said in 2009, which means, white America, he hates *us.* As an indication of how he intends to ex-act his racially motivated revenge, one need look no further, according to Rush Limbaugh, than Zimbabwe, where dictator Robert Mugabe has confiscated white farmers' land. Mugabe, according to Limbaugh, is Obama's "new role model," and "the next thing to look out for is for Obama to take the farms." Because Obama hates white people. Which is no doubt why he put that infamous militant Tim Geithner (a white guy) in charge of the economy and bailed out Wall Street. That'll show us.

From the very beginning of the Obama presiden-cy, famous and influential white people have been try-ing to scare us. First it was Rush, suggesting that the only reason Colin Powell supported Obama was out of racial loyalty; in other words, they're ganging up on us, and we can't trust *any of them*, even the ones we might have thought were OK.

Then there was the steady stream of allegations coming from Fox and talk radio to the effect that organizations like ACORN that are community based (and led mostly by people of color) had tried to steal the election for Obama—it had perhaps even succeeded in doing so—by submitting phony voter registrations in urban precincts. Never mind that there was no evidence of actual fraudulent votes being cast because of ACORN. Never mind that the fraudulent registrations turned in by a handful of ACORN canvassers were caught and reported by the organization itself, as required by law. Never mind that the phony registrations were in the names of cartoon and Disney characters, rendering rather unlikely the possibility that any actual fraud could have transpired—unless, that is, ACORN had some secret plan to get Donald Duck to the polls on Obama's behalf. Regardless of how ridiculous the charges against ACORN were, they were politically brilliant—a way of saying that *those people* are trying to steal the election; they're trying to undermine democracy; they must be stopped.

Then there was the venal attempt on the part of those same voices to blame the nation's economic collapse on progressive lending reforms like the

Community Reinvestment Act (CRA), which seeks to encourage lending in traditionally undercapitalized communities. As the housing bubble began to burst in 2007, conservative commentators pointed a finger at the CRA, blaming it for forcing banks to make loans to "minorities and other risky folks" (as claimed by Fox News commentator Neil Cavuto) despite their inability to pay the notes on their new homes. In other words, it was financial "affirmative action" for the undeserving that was to blame.

Of course, there was no truth to the charge. First, there are no provisions in the CRA that require lending to anyone who can't afford the loan for which they are being approved. Indeed, the law expressly discourages such a thing. Second, the law says nothing about race-based lending whatsoever. There are neither requirements nor even encouragements to direct loans to individuals simply because they happen to be people of color. Third, it was independent mortgage brokers (not even covered by the CRA), who made most of the risky loans that went bad during this period. In fact, only one of the top twenty-five subprime lenders in the nation was required to follow the CRA's strictures, and only 6 percent of all subprime loan dollars were loaned by CRA-covered banks to low-income people whom the law was intended to help. Indeed, loans made under the aegis of the CRA have tended to perform better and have *lower* rates of default and foreclosure than more traditional loans. No, the problem was not lending to poor folks, let alone the poor of color; rather, it was the desire on the part of unscrupulous lenders to make mega-profits off the backs of everyone, by offering risky loans at rates of interest far higher than they should have been. And as one recent study in Louisville discovered, a disproportionate number of the houses that went into foreclosure in largely black urban areas were actually owned by whites in the suburbs who were engaging in real estate speculation, buying up properties in hopes of "flipping" them or deriving rental income. It was the white absentee landlords who failed to pay their notes on time. That people of color (largely renters) were living in the homes did not make the foreclosures their fault; the responsibility for that resided exclusively with those white owners.

Perhaps the biggest issue, unremarked upon by those who would prefer that we blame the darker-hued among our nation's people, was the *deregulation* of mortgage markets, which allowed adjustable-rate mortgages, despite their higher risk; permitted the mixing of commercial and investment banks, despite their much different missions and purposes; and even encouraged devious lenders to price-gouge borrowers with subprime, high-interest loans, knowing full well that the repayment terms would prove onerous for millions.

Additionally, the rise of independent mortgage brokers relied heavily on what is known as an "originate-to-distribute" model of loan underwriting. Under this process, the broker who originates the loan does not keep the loan on their own books (thereby creating an incentive to carefully evaluate the borrower's ability to pay), but rather, sells the loan to others, often larger lending institutions, thereby passing the risk along. During the expanding housing bubble, when people got loans with such an entity, by the time they found themselves unable to pay, the lender would have long since sold the loans to another institution, which was bundling many similar loans into what were called "mortgage-backed securities" intended for re-sale to rich investors. Long before default, the original lending institutions would have been paid its percentage of the initial sale price, and thus had no reason to care whether or not borrowers—again, mostly not poor and not of color—could afford the instruments they were pushing.

But the right won't tell us that, because to put the blame where it belongs, on *deregulation* rather than regulation, on greedy companies and individuals who are of means, rather than poor black and brown people, would hardly serve the right's goal; namely, the manipulation of our racial anxiety and resentments into a potent political weapon.

And in furtherance of that goal the right will say *anything*, including quite a few things even more absurd than the calumnies placed upon the Community Reinvestment Act. Witness the constant drumbeat of rhetoric to the effect that the Obama administration is engaged in a "Nazi-like" takeover of America and perhaps even seeks to "enslave" the people of the nation. Rush Limbaugh, for his part has compared the Obama health care logo to the Nazi swastika and claims that Hitler "ruled by dictate," just "like Barack Obama," and Beck has suggested the administration, by advocating an expansion of community service and volunteer efforts, is really planning on imposing the equivalent of the Nazi SS or Nazi Youth corps.

While such charges may strike the reasonable among us as the very definition of lunacy, there is a *reason* they were made, a logic to them that went unchallenged within the echo chamber that is the American conservative right. Simply put, within a politics of white resentment and victimology, Hitler-laced rants work. After all, Hitler was not just a fascist, but is understood to have been a racial fascist: one whose dictatorial and murderous schemes were directed at a distinctly racialized "other." So to make the black man atop the U.S. political system into Hitler is to plant the idea in white minds that he too will be a *racial* fascist. And if that is the case, the question quite obviously arises, *which race will he be coming for*? Should we be scared? They certainly hope so, and are counting on it.

In addition to those who warn that extermination camps are just around the corner, commentators who are only slightly more reasonable play upon our fears and racial anxieties, too. And so we have Bill O'Reilly—who appears reasonable only in relation to the much more delusional Glenn Beck—claiming, with a straight face, that the nomination of Sonia Sotomayor to the Supreme Court was evidence that the Obama administration believes "white men are the problem in America" and need to be replaced in positions of power by women and folks of color.

Indeed, the Sotomayor nomination brought out the full complement of reactionary bombast, aimed directly at our collective amygdala in an attempt to provoke a new round of racial fears, with Pat Buchanan insisting she was barely literate (although she had graduated from law school, *cum laude*) and was only picked as an affirmative action appointment. Meanwhile, Limbaugh suggested that her support for affirmative action—a position she shares, still, with the slim majority on the Supreme Court—makes her as racist as neo-Nazi David Duke. This, close on the heels of his prior claim that the nomination of the widely respected Eric Holder as Attorney General proved that the only way to get a job in the Obama administration was by "hating white people." And what was the evidence that Holder hated white people? Simple: he dared suggest that Americans—all Americans, not just whites—had long been cowards when it came to discussing race honestly. So if you criticize Americans you hate white people, because Americans and white people are synonymous to the Rush Limbaughs of the world.

No claim is too wild, no allegation of anti-white racial animosity too extreme for the likes of those who would seek to gather us under their right-wing political umbrella, and who have, sadly, already drawn in a large enough percentage of us to be worrisome. Even the passage of a new tax on tanning salon customers was blasted by some in our talk show set as evidence of anti-white animus, since after all, it is mostly white people who use such facilities. The notion that perhaps the Obama administration was actually trying to make tanning more expensive so as to reduce its commonality—and thereby save tens of thousands of us from *deadly skin cancer*—apparently never crossed their minds.

But nothing works better, nor reeks more strongly of racist and crass political opportunism, than the attacks leveled against immigrants of color, mostly from Mexico and other points in the global South, and the way so many within the chattering class (and even the ranks of elected officials) hope to whip us into hysteria about their presence within our shores.

So we have Lou Dobbs, formerly of CNN, insisting that undocumented Mexican migrants are seeking to "reconquer" the American Southwest and, prior to that territorial reclamation, are spreading leprosy throughout the United States. When confronted with the actual data from the Centers for Disease Control utterly eviscerating his fevered claims about disease-spreading Mexicans, Dobbs merely repeated the charge, insisted that he didn't make up the numbers, and went back to *making up the numbers*. Upping the ante further, there were assurances by conservative talking heads like Michael Savage, Neal Boortz and Michelle Malkin to the effect that Mexicans were to blame for the spread of H1N1 "swine flu" in the United States in 2009. Savage even suggested the whole thing was an "al Qaeda plot" to undermine America with crippling viruses brought over the border from Mexico. Forget that the flu didn't actually originate there. In fact, its origins have been traced to hog farms in North Carolina, and date back to 1998. According to the CDC, the viruses were exported from the United States to Asia and then mutated into new forms, which found their way back via an export-import chain linked to the pork industry. Mexico, apparently, had very little to do with anything in the larger international drama. But facts don't matter to those who would whip us into a rabid, immigrant-bashing lather.

Hence their entirely false claims that immigrants, especially those without documentation, are taking our jobs, or soaking up our tax money, and that if we just controlled the border our problems would be over. Forget that migrant flows stimulate consumer demand and actually pump *more* money into the economy—and thus help create jobs and tax revenues—or that closing the border to labor would do nothing to stimulate jobs in the United States, since companies could still take advantage of incentives to locate businesses overseas, or to invest capital there instead of at home.

More to the point, forget the real reasons for increased undocumented migration in the first place: namely, the desperation of low-income persons south of the border, who are struggling in part because of trade agreements initiated by the United States at the behest of corporate interests. Because of agreements like NAFTA, U.S. companies have been able to flood the Mexican market with agricultural goods from the United States (to the benefit of American farmers), which have driven down the price that Mexican farmers are able to garner for crops. This, in turn, causes many of those farmers to leave rural areas in Mexico for work in the cities, but finding the labor market there glutted, they move farther North to support their families—as any of us would do, were we in their shoes. In other words, to whatever extent migrants are crossing the border and thereby (ostensibly) taking other people's jobs, it is only because the economy of Mexico has been considerably undermined by the policies of *our country*. Pathologizing the migrants does nothing to address the real problem and merely serves to drive a wedge between different groups of struggling people, all of whom need better wages and living conditions.

Indeed, if it weren't for the extraordinarily weak labor protections afforded to migrant workers in the United States, companies here would not be nearly so willing or able to take advantage of their desperation. Migrant workers have virtually no rights at all, and certainly none of the protections afforded to native workers, such as minimum-wage protections, overtime benefits, occupational safety and health protections, or protections from racial discrimination. Unlike native-born workers, they have very little if any legal recourse if an employer cheats them out of pay, rendering the undocumented especially vulnerable to unscrupulous bosses. But notice, none of the voices complaining about the flow of so-called illegal immigrants have called for an extension of labor rights and protections to these workers, even though such moves would likely reduce the attractiveness of immigrant labor to profit-seeking business by making it harder for them to take advantage of immigrant desperation. If companies had to pay such workers the same as native-born and documented workers, they would likely hire far fewer of them. But none of the right-wing voices want an extension of labor protections for the undocumented. If anything, they would roll back such protections for all workers, because their concerns are racial, cultural and economic, and have nothing to do with the well-being of workers, white or otherwise.

So rather than address those core issues relevant to all workers in the hemisphere—especially the way global capital has played brown folks and black folks off against one another, and against most of us—we get scapegoating. So we have Arizona passing a law that essentially legalizes and even mandates racial and ethnic profiling by requiring that law officers stop and question anyone they might reasonably suspect is in the country illegally. Reasonable suspicion, of course, means whatever police *say* it means. Most anything can be interpreted as reasonably suspicious. So, for instance, if an officer sees Latinos speaking Spanish in a public place, or hanging out, speaking to someone in a parked vehicle, they might presume these people to be undocumented day laborers illegally looking for employment. Under the law, cracking down on such work is to be especially prioritized, so there is every reason to believe such indicators of suspicion would lead to widespread harassment of persons whose only real crime was being Spanish-speaking, brown-skinned and, from all appearances, working-class. Honestly now, do we really believe that white folks from European nations, speaking with accents, are going to be questioned under this law?

The truth is, the Arizona law (which is currently on hold pending judicial review) and almost all anti-immigrant hysteria is about race, no matter how loudly and unconvincingly those pushing the agenda try to deny it. I know that many of us claim this isn't true, that instead they merely seek to crack down on those who enter the nation without proper documentation. "If they would just come legally," many insist, they would have no problem with immigration. But it's difficult to accept the veracity of the claim. After all, were it merely a matter of process there would be an easy solution, which I'm guessing most would be loath to support: we could just make coming to the nation legally as easy as filling out a postcard—perhaps even with one's fingerprint, just for the sake of argument—mailing it in and waiting a week for a background check, after which, assuming the check came back normal, the applicant would be legal. Voila! There would be hardly any more undocumented crossings—most everyone, after all, would be willing to wait seven days to do it safely and legally. But no one ever suggests this solution, or anything remotely like it, which seems clearly to indicate that the real problem is less about the distinction between documented and undocumented immigrants, and more about the mere fact of brown-skinned migration in the first place. Many of us simply don't want particular people, no matter the manner in which they come.

Of course, who can blame us for being nervous about the infusion of large numbers of Latinos? With the right insisting that the Ethnic Studies program in the Tucson Unified School District (which has dramatically boosted Latino graduation rates and the rates at which such students go to college) is teaching Chicanos and Chicanas to "hate white people," one can understand our anxiety. If we teach *the truth* about U.S. history and the way that Latino and Latina folk have been marginalized by white supremacy, they may end up hating us; so we must end such classes, and rewrite the textbooks used across the nation—as has been proposed in Texas and Tennessee by conservative activists masquerading as history scholars—so as to minimize the discussions of racism and injustice perpetrated against people of color. We mustn't talk about such things, not because they aren't true, but because the truths they address are too incendiary to be entrusted to impressionable young people. Naturally, we will not likely apply the same concerns to teaching about 9/11—we will not, to be sure, refuse to speak of *that* in schools out of a concern that it might encourage some folks to hate Arabs or Muslims or both—but in the instant case, and with regard to Mexicans, ignorance is strength, and history a mere speed bump on the patriotic highway.

∞

Nothing, of course, serves to inflate uncritical nationalistic hubris like nostalgia, nor does anything else so perfectly play to white fears concerning a changing nation, and it is this commodity, nostalgic reverence for the America of old, in which the right consistently traffics. From Glenn Beck's nightly television paeans to the "good old days" of "innocence" long since ravaged by the forces of liberal darkness to Pat Buchanan's lament that "traditional Americans" (wonder what *they* look like?) are losing "their" country, we are regularly subjected to the insistence that somehow the nation has lost its way, and that the changes afoot are to the detriment of all that "real Americans" should hold dear.

The nostalgia project has two components, equally important for rallying the angry and disaffected among us to a political cause: first, the Pollyanna-like glorification of the nation's past, and second, the sanitizing of whatever parts of that past might strike a discordant note of contradiction in the retelling of the national narrative.

On the glorification front, consider the words of presidential candidate and conservative favorite Michele Bachmann, who recently bragged about growing up in "John Wayne's America," and whose comments suggested a longing for a return to those days. Or Glenn Beck, who serves as the would-be conductor on the train back to Pleasantville, and who in 2009 became weepy at two classic commercials played during his television show: commercials that make him especially wistful for those good old days about which he is so emotional.

One in particular is worth noting: a Kodak spot from 1975 featuring the song "Times of Your Life," by Paul Anka, piped over old Super-8 footage of families from the 1950s and 1960s. No question, it was an effective and touching ad. But in the hands of Beck, it became something else. Rather than seeing the spot as what it was (an emotion-laden manipulation intended to sell products and make Kodak a lot of money), Beck presented it as a literal nod to national unity and togetherness. While acknowledging that "America has always had her problems"—the typical, obscenely understated way in which white conservatives tend to gloss over things like apartheid and institutionalized racial supremacy—Beck insisted that once upon a time (like back in the days represented by that commercial) "we used to be united on some basic things."

"Do you remember how that felt?" Beck queried his viewers. "Do you remember what life was like?" he continued. And then, in his crowning challenge, he speculated that if a politician promised he could take us back to those "simpler times," when the flowers presumably smelled better, the skies were bluer and even one's tears tasted like molasses (presuming for a minute that one would ever have occasion to cry in a place as blissful as this), we would all "do it in a heartbeat." "Wouldn't ya?" he added with the "aw shucks" earnestness that has become his hallmark.

All of which suggests that Beck doesn't actually remember much, or perhaps never learned much, about those days. What unity could he possibly be speaking about, after all? Would it be the unity of the 1950s, which led our parents and grandparents to so gladly embrace the *Brown v. Board of Education* decision, requiring the desegregation of previously all-white schools? The unity that prompted our forebears, in the wake of that ruling, to all rush to the local florist, purchase bouquets and hand them out to black children as a welcome to their new educational environs?

Perhaps he meant the unity that led Montgomery, Alabama, bus operators to help Ms. Rosa Parks to her seat up front and chastise that one unruly white guy who, owing to his own mistaken assumptions that the town was something *other* than unified behind the notion of civil rights, thought blacks were still supposed to be relegated to the back of the bus?

Or the unity that in 1963 led every single white person in America to attend the March on Washington to demand the passage of civil rights legislation, which, oddly, was going to be passed anyway on a unanimous vote, seeing as how everyone was unified behind "some basic things," like equal rights for all.

Come to think of it, perhaps he meant the part where everyone loved Dr. King, and so the FBI never spied on him, and when he condemned the slaughter in Vietnam by saying that the United States had become the "greatest purveyor of violence in the world today," everyone applauded his courage, since they had all said it before themselves. And of course it was really great how no one ever killed him, because all were so united in their admiration.

To proclaim that America was *ever* unified, at least behind much of anything important, is to ignore the whole of the national experience. Even during World War Two, arguably the most unified period in our national life, black veterans viewed the campaign against European fascism and Japanese imperialism different- ly. But it is doubtful that Beck or his listeners have ever heard of the "Double-V" (for victory) campaign, which saw the war effort as existing on both foreign and do- mestic fronts: in Europe, in Asia *and* at home, against the racial oppression to which veterans of color were being subjected and would continue to be subjected even after their triumphant return.

And while our people chose as heroes soldiers like Audie Murphy or draft-dodging but oh-so-masculine actors like Michele Bachmann's John Wayne—who actually got out of service to allow for the furtherance of his movie career—black folks cleaved to an entirely different set of role models: from the Tuskegee airmen (about whom most of us knew little for more than a generation), to the martyrs of the civil rights movement, white and of color: people like the Reverend George Lee, Vernon Dahmer, Medgar Evers, Wharlest Jackson, Herbert Lee, Sammy Younge Jr., Andrew Goodman, Michael Schwerner, James Chaney, Harriette Moore, Jimmie Lee Jackson, Lamar Smith, James Reeb, William Moore, Jonathan Daniels and Viola Liuzzo, among others. That few of us have even heard these names (and that the history books used for teaching all Americans rarely mention them) suggests that, as with Beck, the culture in general would rather gloss over the evidence of disunity that has marked us from the beginning, would prefer to fabricate a commonality of purpose and vision that has never existed anywhere within the borders of the nation we call home.

No, most of us prefer to dwell in an entirely fictive

place, a *Leave It to Beaver* or *Andy Griffith* fantasyland, where Opie Taylor casts lines down at the ol' fishin' hole with "Pa" and the experiences of racial others are ignored, forgotten, relegated to the backwaters of memory. Those other experiences we treat as if they were shown on some giant Etch-a-Sketch, which we can conveniently erase with a vigorous shake or two, obliterating all evidence of the inadequacies made visible by the work of our own hands.

Which then brings us to the second element in the nostalgic political project upon which the right has embarked, and in which they hope, sincerely, to enlist our participation; namely, the rewriting of history to sanitize the racist horrors visited upon millions of our brothers and sisters. Those who would engage in the whitewash are fully aware that many of us are quite open to the deception. The fact is, we have tried hard over the years not to hear the voices of those who have borne the brunt of systemic exclusion and marginalization. In effect, we have placed noise-canceling headphones over our ears, letting in only the pleasant sounds *we* wish to hear, while shutting out the rest. So the dulcet tones of patriotism, the self-congratulatory rhythms of American exceptionalism have soothed us to the point of inducing a collective coma, a hypnotic state of perpetual positivity. Meanwhile, the harsh and discordant notes and backbeats of racism and discrimination have been kept from our consciousness, drowned out by far happier melodies.

So we have the aforementioned Michele Bachmann insisting that the nation's history of racial oppression really wasn't that bad. The founders, for instance, worked "tirelessly" to end enslavement, according to Bachmann. Forget that most of them owned other human beings and never even managed to "work tirelessly" to free their own, let alone end the larger system of enslavement that kept them chained as property; or that they wrote into the Constitution specific protections for slave owners, including clauses requiring that runaways be returned to their masters. Forget that whole Civil War thing (which transpired roughly half a century after most all the founders were dead), or the slave rebellions that helped undermine the system, or the John Brown raid. The founders were racially enlightened good guys, sayeth the former tax attorney from Minnesota. Indeed, when Congress decided to read the Constitution on the House floor shortly after the Republican Party took control in 2010—largely to mollify those in the Tea Party movement who insist they seek a return to Constitutional principles—they deliberately *excised* all portions of the document referring to slavery, as if to suggest that such a thing never happened, or that if it did, it wasn't worth reflecting upon. Better to uncritically remember the genius of the founders, or to believe, as Bachmann apparently does, that they fashioned a nation in which "it didn't matter the color of your skin."

And let's not forget that George Washington "loved the Indians," according to Glenn Beck, never mind that he waged an annihilationist war against them. Indeed, Washington wrote to Major General John Sullivan, imploring him to "lay waste" to all Iroquois settlements, so that their lands may not be "merely overrun but destroyed."

Speaking of native peoples, what must they think as they listen to so many of us insisting that it is improper to allow the construction of a Muslim cultural center a few blocks from the site of the 9/11 attacks? That argument, after all—with which the majority of us seem to agree, according to polls—rests upon the notion that "Ground Zero" is virtually sacred land, and that to allow a Muslim center (and, God forbid, a mosque, as many mistakenly called it) would be to defile the memories of those who died as a result of Muslim extremism there. But as any indigenous North American can tell you, there is scarcely a square foot of land on which we tread that is not, for someone, Ground Zero. I am sitting atop one now as I write these words: a killing field for Cherokee, Chickasaw, Choctaw and Creek; a graveyard in which are buried the bones of peoples whose holocaust occurred not so long ago and is still remembered by those who have not the luxury of forgetting. We haven't prohibited the construction of churches all over that land, just because the church and Christianity served as instruments of that evisceration.

It takes some nerve and a disturbing sense of entitlement to believe that our pain is the only pain that counts, that only *our* ground zero matters and should be memorialized in this way, or to suggest that we are the only ones who have known terror, and that having done so we now have the right to draw a circle around us, a bubble of specialness that can keep us warm and protected like some amniotic sac inside which we will forever be insulated from harm. But that is what our nostalgic and completely inaccurate remembrance of history practically guarantees: it allows us to rewrite the past and erase from our memories those aspects in which we come up a bit short in the greatness department.

Anyone who dares reflect accurately upon that history is made a pariah for daring to question the nostalgic narrative. According to the right, for instance, Supreme Court Justice Elena Kagan is to be condemned because she dared concur with the opinion of former Justice Thurgood Marshall, for whom she once clerked. And what was Marshall's opinion, the concurrence with which would invite such shrieks of indignation on the part of those out to discredit her? Simple: it was the part about how the nation, as originally conceived, was "defective from the start," due to its enshrinement of enslavement and white supremacy. This is a position with which no intellectually honest or remotely informed person could disagree, but with which, apparently, millions of us do. Which says *nothing* about Thurgood Marshall or Elena Kagan, but volumes about those who would criticize either on this point.

But what can we expect, in a nation where the likes of former Senator (and now Republican presidential candidate) Rick Santorum can chastise President Obama for making the point that America didn't really begin to come into its promise until after the civil rights revolution of the 1960s and the creation of certain social programs like Medicare and Medicaid, intended to provide a modicum of health security to the American public? As Santorum recently bellowed on the campaign trail, America was a "great place before 1965," a statement which is not even remotely true, and which stands as a slap in the face to every person of color who resided here before that time. Before 1965, this country was a system of formal white supremacy and institutionalized apartheid. It was not even decent, let alone great, for millions of Americans. That it had the potential for greatness is inarguable, but that is neither what Santorum said nor what he intended to suggest. He intended to obliterate, by his comments, the lived experiences of people of color, about whom he apparently could not care less. *His* memories of the past, and ours (as white folks), are the ones that matter to him.

So too with Mike Huckabee, formerly the Governor of Arkansas and a Fox News personality, who has criticized the president for "not seeing America" the way "we do," and specifically because while Obama was living in places like Indonesia for a brief period, or Hawaii (doing God knows what), "we" were going to Boy Scout and Rotary Club meetings. *Really?* We were? Who was? Not black folks on the South Side of Chicago. Not Latinos in East L.A. Not Lakota people on Pine Ridge. For that matter, not even most of *us* were living that small-town, Mayberry, cornpone kind of life. But by saying it, by suggesting that the *real* America is different from Obama's America—and for that matter, folks of color generally, or urban types more broadly—Huckabee can play directly to that sense of national glory squandered, national identity under attack, and the need for some type of small-town (implicitly white) rebirth.

Upon close reflection the attempt is transparent, but sadly, close reflection on such matters is not what we're encouraged to engage in. Rather, those who brandish nostalgia as a political tool know that for people who are anxious, nervous about cultural, political, economic and demographic change, this kind of thing works. It primes the pump of racial insecurity, making it that much easier for those so primed to stand and declare their desire, above all else, to "take their country back."

∞

Of course I know that many of us white folk get upset at this suggestion—at the notion that this mantra of national reclamation is somehow connected to a narrative of racial nostalgia or resentment. Two years ago I engaged in a rather lengthy email exchange with someone whose views no doubt mirrored those of many millions more. She was upset because of something I had said during a television interview on CNN regarding the Tea Party movement. Being a part of that movement, she took offense to what she perceived to be my position; namely, that the Tea Party was propelled forward by racial hatred of a black president. I tried to explain that, in fact, that was not my argument. I do not believe that the Tea Party movement, or its individual members and supporters, are operating necessarily out of racist motivations, nor have I ever claimed that opposition to the president automatically or even necessarily makes one racist. I had said, however, and do believe that the mantra of taking the country "back" contains an unhealthy degree of racial resentment as part of its "background noise." It isn't racism in the classic sense; rather, it is the rhetoric of white anxiety operationalized in a political movement. When white people—and especially older white people—speak of going "back" to an earlier time, it is not unreasonable to become a bit nervous about what they might mean. I know the kind of country that was theirs as children and young adults.

The difference between racism and racial resentment was lost on her, and she continued to press her case. Race had *nothing* to do with the Tea Party movement, she insisted. The desire to take the country back is not about segregation, she assured me, not about going back to the days of overt racial oppression and Jim Crow. So I decided to play the game, and asked her quite simply what the Tea Party folks mean when they say they wish to "take their country back?" What *is* that about, if it's not about race? Simple, she said: we mean that we want to go back to a time of lower taxes and smaller government. And more to the point, we'd like to return to a time when people were self-sufficient and didn't rely on others to provide for them—when people believed in taking personal responsibility for their lives. This, she explained, was the kind of self-reliance that was directly at stake in the health care debate. If health care reform passed—even the minimalist reforms proposed by the Obama administration, which would have fallen far short of a guaranteed national health care system—the rugged individualism that had long marked our nation's culture would be destroyed. People would become ever more dependent on others to take care of them, rather than relying on their own initiative and hard work.

I suspect that many of you who consider yourselves conservatives—and even some who aren't that far to the right—would echo her sentiments in this regard. Such conservatism, you might say, is largely about a philosophical belief in limited government intervention in the economic workings of the nation—a preference for individual self-sufficiency and independence—and a tax burden less onerous than what you experience today. So far so good. But might we dig a bit deeper? Because when we do, we begin to notice that the debate about the size and scope of government, about taxation, about "individualism" versus the "collective good," has been implicitly about race for several years now. It is not merely a philosophical issue but an intensely racialized discourse.

Take taxes for example. The Tea Partier insisted to me that she wanted to go back to a time when taxes were lower. Yet she failed to specify when that might be. I wanted to know exactly when in our nation's history did she think we had more or less gotten it right when it came to the proper level of taxation, and so I asked her. Now, I suppose she could have said 1897, or 1909. Both were before the imposition of the federal income tax, and in relative terms, I suppose they were periods of "low taxation." But I knew she wouldn't say either of these. Children were working in factories and mines in those days, workers had no rights whatsoever, and unless you were one of a handful of rich white people or their kids, life was pretty rough. She could have said 1926, I suppose. Although this was after the imposition of the income tax, the rates of taxation were relatively low on most people, so was that perhaps, what she meant? But of course not. The 1920s were rather miserable for most folks: not just people of color suffering under the weight of racial apartheid, but most whites as well, whose economic and social condition left more than a little to be desired.

As it turns out, when I had asked her the question—when I had asked her to give me a year that was, in her mind, emblematic of a time when taxes had been at their proper level and the size of government appropriate—but before she had had the chance to write me back, I had scribbled a note on a piece of paper on my desk. It was a note meant to serve as a guess, on my part, as to what she would say. I've never been much of a gambler, but had there been a bookie prepared to take bets on the answer she was going to give me, I could have cleaned up, because I nailed it.

The answer came back in a matter of minutes: 1957.

It was a fascinating answer, because it just so happens that in 1957 the top marginal tax rate in the United States was *ninety-one percent*. In other words, after a certain income level—which in those days was $200,000 for a single person, and $400,000 for a married couple—ninety-one cents of every additional dollar earned was taken by the government: more than double the highest rate in existence today, even if all the recent tax cuts were allowed to expire. There were actually *eighteen* tax brackets in 1957 that were higher than anything we have today, and corporate taxes were much higher then, as a share of overall revenue and as a share of the larger economy. So to say that the nation needs to go back to the mid-to-late 1950s because that was a time of lower taxes makes no sense whatsoever. It suggests that there must be something other than the tax burden of that time which makes individuals like those in the Tea Party so wistful. Might that "something else" be related to the white-dominated racial hierarchy that existed during those days?

Many might argue that she just didn't realize—and perhaps many on the right simply were unaware—that the tax rates had been so high in those days. Might not such people be operating merely from ignorance as opposed to racial resentment? Maybe, but again, let's dig a bit deeper. Why, after all, might so many people remember the pre-1960 decades as a time of lower taxation? Why is it so common (and it really *is* quite common) to perceive the era before the 1960s as an era before the explosion of taxes and government spending? Is it because the people who perceive the 1960s and beyond as a time of onerous taxation are reflecting critically on the space program, or the taxes raised to finance the Vietnam War, or the rising defense budgets of the 1980s? Surely not. I think we know what comes to mind when one mentions the 1960s, especially when we think of that decade in relation to government programs for which taxes may have been used. And I think we know, white America, if we allow ourselves to be honest, the color of the people we perceive to be the beneficiaries of all that taxation, and the color of the victims of the same.

Which then brought us to the part about "smaller government." She had said after all, that the conservative desire to "take the country back" meant no more than the desire to limit the degree of government intervention in our daily economic lives. But government had not been small prior to the 1960s, far from it. For whites it had always been huge, in fact, and we rather liked it that way. Although the debate about the size of government has been a long-standing one, dating back to the earliest days of the republic, for almost the entire national history, it was a debate between political and economic elites. Some believed in a more activist government and some believed in a far smaller one, but the persons lining up to participate in that argument were always those at the pinnacle of the social order. Among average everyday folks—workaday peoples—there was *never* much of a debate about this matter. Working-class folks, including virtually all working-class white folks, believed without a doubt in the necessity and legitimacy of government intervention in the economy to help those in need, to create opportunities and to make lives better.

That's why, white America, we had no objection to (and indeed supported mightily) the "big government" intervention known as the Homestead Act, passed in 1862, which gave over 200 million acres of essentially "free" land to white families: land that had been confiscated from indigenous people or from Mexico and was then made available to white settlement. Millions of us today still live on that land, procured thanks to government intervention, or we have in some way benefited from the sale of that land and the passing down of the assets intergenerationally; and I haven't seen one among us go to Washington and, in a fit of self-conscious embarrassment, offer to give back the house, the ranch, the farm or the money gleaned from their sale, out of a concern that were we to keep them we might be partaking in a form of socialism.

Likewise, average, everyday white folks had no objection to (and indeed, supported quite stridently) the New Deal programs of the 1930s. The rich didn't like them much, as they offered poor people alternatives to exploitative pay in the private market—whether government jobs or various forms of social insurance to serve as a safety net for the desperate—but among the masses they were almost uniformly popular.

Average everyday white folks loved the Federal Housing Administration (FHA) home loan program, and later the Veterans Administration (VA) home loan programs—both huge government interventions in the workings of the private housing market—and with good reason: they were largely responsible (along with the GI Bill—another big government initiative) for creating the American middle class. The FHA and VA programs alone financed over $120 billion in home equity for our people from 1934 to 1962, and by 1960 were responsible for nearly half of all white mortgages in the country. And we loved the Interstate Highway program—more big government—because it made long-distance travel on the open road possible for so many of us, and because it made it easier for us to run to the suburbs, where only we could live, and which were being created thanks to low-cost, government-subsidized loans.

In other words, for most of the nation's history, white folks like the ones participating in Tea Party rallies—average, somewhat middling white people—absolutely *loved* government intervention. But somewhere along the way, things changed. And when that change happened (and why) is the critical point for us to interrogate, for it tells us a lot about how race has influenced even philosophical matters that seem at first glance to have nothing to do with it.

Almost all of those big government programs I just mentioned, which retained such high levels of support from the white masses, had been racially exclusive in design and implementation. In fact, the only way President Roosevelt could get most of the New Deal passed was by capitulating to the racist whims of white Southern senators who insisted that blacks be excluded from most of its benefits. Social Security was, in effect, racially exclusionary for its first twenty years, thanks to language that blocked agricultural workers or domestic workers—about 80 percent of the black workforce—from participating. The FHA program operated with underwriting guidelines that essentially kept anyone who wasn't white from receiving the government-guaranteed loans for the first thirty years of its existence. Even the GI Bill, theoretically open to all returning veterans, worked in a racially discriminatory way, with persons of color far less likely to receive substantial job or educational opportunities under its aegis than our people were. Employers and colleges were allowed to exclude people of color from their ranks, no matter the latter groups' "right" to use GI Bill benefits; hence those veterans of color who could make use of the benefits were still relegated to the lowest-rung employment opportunities and limited to a small number of potential educational institutions.

In other words, government had always been big for people like us, and we were fine with that. But beginning in the 1960s, as people of color began to gain access to the benefits for which we had always been eligible, suddenly we discovered our inner libertarian and decided that government intervention was bad, perhaps even the cause of social decay and irresponsible behavior on the part of those who reaped its largesse. Indeed, even cash welfare—created as part of the 1935 Social Security Act—was originally supported as a way to help white women whose husbands had died or left home to look for work during the Depression, so they could stay home, raise their kids, and not have to work in the paid labor force. Interesting isn't it? Cash welfare was originally conceived and defended on these grounds: as a way to foster benign dependence on the state. And virtually no one balked. But as soon as women of color gained access to the same benefits, those programs came to be seen as the cause of all that was wrong with the poor. They made you lazy, encouraged you to have babies out of wedlock (forget that the states with the most generous welfare programs always had the lowest rates of such births), and needed to be cut back, perhaps even eliminated.

Doesn't it seem convenient that growing opposition to government intervention in the economy, the housing market, the job market and other aspects of American life parallels almost directly the racialization of social policy, and the increasing association in the white mind between such efforts and handouts to the undeserving "other"? Are we to believe that this correlation is merely coincidental? That people who had long reaped the benefits of big government simply came to a deeper understanding of the inherent dangers of such a thing, only *after* they had ridden the wave of such benefits for generations? Surely we can't expect anyone to believe that. No, the backlash against government was directly related to the increasingly common belief that *those people* were abusing the programs. And so, beginning in the early 1970s—even as antipoverty efforts had helped bring down poverty rates by roughly half between 1960 and 1973, and by a third in just the first eight years of the Great Society programs—safety net programs began to be cut, or frozen in place, their benefits eroded by inflation over the years, guaranteeing that whatever potential they had to work would be eroded as well.

So it isn't that opposition to an activist government is racist *per se*. There are surely many of us who would stake out the limited government position even in a society where everyone looked the same. But in *this* society, where the debate about the size and scope of government has been intrinsically bound up with the debate about race—and the negative perceptions of racial others—it is patently impossible to suggest with any intellectual integrity that the two can be fully separated. That is why the Tea Party narrative, and the narrative of the American right, is properly considered one of white racial resentment and anxiety.

But getting back to my email correspondence with the Tea Party member, let us explore the last of her claims. It is one with which many would perhaps agree, to the effect that the country has somehow (in just the past few years of the Obama administration) been led away from the notion of individual responsibility, and down the road of dependency. Perhaps many would echo her view that we've lost our way, that America has forgotten the importance of personal responsibility, and so things like publicly supported health care programs are a dangerous imposition on an otherwise straightforward national narrative of individualism.

But putting aside how that belief clearly fails to jibe with the long history of government intervention in the economy—which intervention was, again, supported by the vast majority of white Americans—there is this larger and perhaps more uncomfortable truth: At no point have we who are white been particularly enamored of the concept of independence and hard work. We have *always* been dependent, and have always relied on others to help us, however much we've managed to craft a fictional narrative about our self-reliance and sell that to the world as if it were real. And on a racial level, we have certainly been far more dependent on people of color than they've ever been on us. I know it's a touchy subject, but the history is really quite clear, and worth remembering.

We depended on the indigenous of this land to teach us farming and harvesting skills that we largely lacked upon arrival. Indeed, had it not been for the wisdom of native North Americans, the first attempt at European colonization would have failed entirely. We were starving in droves, perishing in Jamestown because we had spent so much time looking for gold that we'd forgotten to plant crops that could sustain us through the harsh winters. Four hundred–plus years later that folly has been repeated, at least metaphorically, in an economy so focused on the chasing of wealth for wealth's sake that it has failed to re-sow its crops, to invest in the future, to actually produce anything of value as it opts, instead, to chase financial fortunes and immediate riches.

We relied on the slave labor of African peoples to build the levees that protected our homes and farmland, to harvest and cook our food, to care for our children, to chop, and hoe, and sweat, and sew, and nurse us back to health, while we aspired to be persons of leisure, or at least to leave the really brutal work to them.

For a visceral example of what I mean, I really do recommend that you take a trip to the Nottoway Plantation, located on Louisiana Highway 1, along the Mississippi River between New Orleans and Baton Rouge. Known as the "White Castle" by the family of John Hampden Randolph, for whom it was constructed, Nottoway and its history—about which the tour guides will gladly speak without the least sense of irony—stands as a testament to white dependency and incompetence, however obscured by great wealth and power.

Randolph grew rich as a producer of cotton and then sugar, relying in large part on the mortgaging of slaves he had inherited from his own family and that of his wife, so as to establish the plantation at Nottoway. Once established, the plantation and another he owned ultimately held in bondage as many as four hundred persons of African descent. Without the labor of those he enslaved he could not likely have made a go of the land for one week, given as he was to spending his time hunting and going for long rides in carriages, or hosting parties for others of the elite with whom he associated—this according not to me, but to the official plantation website history. That his leisurely indulgences and utter lack of personal work ethic do not cause us to perhaps reconsider the rugged individualism upon which we are told white men have always relied, should tell us something about both that mythology and the white men in whose service it has been so regularly employed.

In any event, Nottoway was a manse with sixty-four rooms in all, including its most unique and striking—a ballroom for dances and other high society events, washed in bright white paint from floor to ceiling. Each of the dozen Randolph children was assigned a personal servant—this is how the docents put it, but in truth we are talking about chattel, make no mistake—and when the children needed to call one of their "servants" (perhaps to feed them, clean up after them or wipe their behinds after a particularly difficult bowel movement), they could use for the purpose a bell system rigged to levers in each room, the levers connected by string to bells on the servants' "waiting porch," as it was called. There were *dozens* of different bell tones, each one signaling that help was needed in a particular room. Of course, those enslaved by the Randolphs, who were thought to be the intellectual inferiors of those whom they served, had to know exactly which bell went to which room, so as to make sure they could come quickly in case one of the Randolph brood needed assistance with something they could never, naturally, be expected to do for themselves. That a family would go to such lengths to avoid *work*—even the effort required to simply go and *find* the black person whose help they needed so badly, rather than to simply flick a lever and thereby exert no more effort than might have been be required to pick one's own nose—may stand as the most exquisite example of laziness in the history of either white people or slackers (histories that have tended to overlap considerably, especially at the upper end of the wealth spectrum)

Once slavery was abolished and Randolph had to actually pay for the labor on his property—which is to say, once he had to make a go of it without the unfair edge of government intervention on his behalf, helping him to hold human beings in bondage—he failed miserably, ultimately losing most of his fortune and three-fourths of his accumulated acreage. Though he tried to maintain the plantation's former greatness—this time with Chinese labor, signaling once again an inability of the white and wealthy to do anything themselves—he could never recapture the antebellum glories to which he and his family had grown accustomed.

And it wasn't only the wealthy among us who grew dependent on people of color; no indeed, even working-class whites often employed blacks leased out by slave owners, or in other ways relied on their free labor to build up the economy from which they too benefited, if not nearly so much as the wealthy. The condition of black and brown labor marked the economic floor to which no white worker would be allowed to fall, an assurance that propped up white workers in relative terms and gave us a stake (however ultimately inadequate) in the system of white supremacy.

Beyond that, all whites depended on laws to defend slavery and segregation so as to elevate us politically, socially and economically. We were dependent on Mexicans to teach us how to extract gold from river-beds and quartz—critical to the growth of the economy in the mid-to-late 1800s—and had we not taken over half their nation in an unprovoked war, the Pacific ports so vital to the modern U.S. economy would have been not ours, but Mexico's. Then we were dependent on their labor in the mid-twentieth century under the *bracero* program, through which more than five million Mexicans were brought into the country for agricultural work, and then sent back across the border. And we were dependent on Asian labor to build the railroads that made transcontinental commerce possible. Ninety percent of the labor used to build the Central Pacific Railroad in the 1860s was Chinese, imported for the purpose, and exploited because the rail bosses felt that group was easier to control than white workers.

Indeed, our dependence on people of color continues to this day. Each year, African Americans alone spend over $700 billion with white-owned companies: money that goes mostly into the pockets of white owners, white employees, white stockholders and the white communities in which they live. Even the mass incarceration of people of color (largely for nonviolent drug-related offenses) has resulted in the transfer of billions of dollars to white communities—money upon which those communities have come to depend. Because prisons are typically located in small, mostly white places, and because inmates count in the local community's population numbers, their transfer from large cities to rural prisons results in more federal funds for rural communities due to census-based budgetary allocations: up to $25,000 per inmate. And, of course, undocumented immigrants of color, about whom we make so much fuss, pump billions of additional dollars into the economy, well beyond the value of whatever benefits they manage to wrangle, in education, health care or other social services.

So make no mistake, the narrative of individualism

and personal responsibility bears little resemblance to the reality of our lives, as a nation or as a people. Support from the state, and specifically *racialized* state policy and racially exclusive government intervention on our behalf, has been the norm. It's not that we haven't worked hard. Most of us have and do, every day. But some folks' hard work has been rewarded by access to an opportunity structure, while the hard work of others has been largely ignored, and certainly not rewarded with the same access. And that has made a difference.

∞

Many of you may think all of this an academic matter, but it goes far beyond that. As conservatives abuse historical memory and take advantage of our anxieties and fears about a changing society in order to push their own agenda, the risks to the nation grow ever greater. And ironically, the likelihood that the very real insecurity many of us are currently experiencing—and even the very real economic pain we are feeling—will ever be addressed becomes more remote. This is the dirty little secret about which the right would have us remain unaware: they are selling us scapegoats and bogeymen, none of whom are really responsible for our plight, rather than dealing with the very real causes of our present troubles.

And so they will seek to discredit the notion of the public good, whether represented by guaranteed health care access or publicly supported economic stimulus and job creation programs, and instead insist on budget cuts, forgetting the fact that millions of us are out of work too, and lack affordable health care. Yet many of us fall for it, openly admitting on camera that we'd rather go without health care than have it provided by the government. But how many of us would continue to feel that way when in need of care after surviving a heart attack, or at the very moment when our spouse or partner or a parent suffered an exploding brain aneurism, or the next time one of our children has a fever of 105 and goes into convulsions? In the face of those harsh realities, how many of us would continue to insist upon the evil of big government, were we devoid of adequate private insurance?

No matter how much we've been encouraged to ignore it, the fact remains that the public good is *our* good, for we are part of the public too. And unless we can see the fates of all those black and brown folks that the right has been encouraging us to fear and loathe as our brothers and sisters, we're in for some rough years ahead. Indeed, had we allowed ourselves to see the commonality of interests early on—and this is the truly sick thing, the thing that should *really* keep us up at night—the pain and anxiety so many of our number are currently experiencing may never have manifested at all.

For instance, consider the current housing meltdown. Although the crisis is now being felt nationwide, in communities that are urban, suburban and rural, and by people across the color spectrum, things weren't always that way. More than fifteen years ago, Michael Hudson detailed in his groundbreaking book *Merchants of Misery* the way that poor folks—mostly of color—were being gouged by high-interest lenders on the secondary mortgage market, thanks to discriminatory practices. Likewise, in the late 1990s and early 2000s community-based groups in places like North Carolina were taking on predatory lenders like Citi, which was caught charging black families hundreds of thousands of dollars in additional mortgage payments over the life of their loans, steering them into loan instruments that were more costly than necessary even when those families could have qualified for lower interest rates.

For years prior to that time, lenders had been notorious for "redlining" low-income communities (especially those of color)—literally drawing lines around entire census tracts on city maps, prohibiting lending to anyone within the line, no matter their individual creditworthiness—and thereby starving whole neighborhoods of needed capital investment, wealth and stable home ownership. As a result, by the early

1990s such communities had been made so desperate by these policies that they were ripe for abuse by "reverse redlining," in which lenders targeted people living there for loans (albeit at high interest). Had lending been balanced and fair from the start, the targeted communities would not have been in such dire straits to begin with, and families would have been less vulnerable to the enticements of unscrupulous lenders preying on their desire to take part in the "American dream" of home ownership.

Yet consistently, when activists would raise these issues, decry the racial and class unfairness inherent to these practices and call for regulations, most of the media, public and lawmakers, and most of *us* routinely ignored them. No national politicians campaigned on platforms to crack down on such policies, to strengthen fair lending laws, or to rein in the interest that lenders could charge. The market, they would insist, was sufficient to regulate these matters.

Of course, once it became apparent that lenders were not going to be heavily scrutinized or regulated when it came to these activities, high-cost mortgage instruments became even more prevalent, and began to spread from the communities of color and poor communities, where they had begun, to solidly middle-class and largely white spaces too. As a result of the spread of high-cost mortgages, folks in middle-class and mostly white counties like Suffolk and Nassau, on Long Island, are now facing higher foreclosure rates than residents in Brooklyn or Queens. Although the overall impact of the busted housing bubble continues to fall most heavily on people of color—indeed, the wealth gains of the past thirty years by African Americans have been all but wiped out by the collapse—the rot is spreading, to be sure, and many of us are finding ourselves vulnerable in ways we could never have imagined.

So in a very real sense, our ambivalence to the suffering of black and brown folks opened the floodgates to even more risky economic activity, and this time, in the very places where so many of us live. Had racial inequity and injustice been seen as a problem early on, perhaps the market for such predatory loans would have been shut down or at least heavily regulated, thereby staving off crisis. Clearly, millions of us who got roped into these instruments by lenders promising that everything would be all right are suffering today precisely because the pain was not taken seriously when it belonged to someone else. Not to mention that even if our own neighborhoods and communities haven't been hammered by the collapse, and even if we're having no problems paying our mortgages, the credit crunch that has resulted from the larger crisis can affect our ability to refinance, sell our own homes or buy new property. In short, the housing collapse hurts most all of us, and it was the indifference to the pain when localized in black and brown communities that helped bring us to this point.

Additionally, there is now a significant body of research suggesting that the reason the United States has such a feeble social safety net—a weak system of unemployment insurance, limited cash-based support, paltry food subsidies, inadequate public health care initiatives—is due to the perception on the part of large numbers of us that black folks will abuse such programs if they are too generous. In other words, our racial resentment of folks of color (perceived as the ones taking advantage of any form of assistance for the needy) leads to less support for strong safety net programs. Yet when the economy craters and millions of us find ourselves struggling to survive, we too end up without the programs needed to support our families.

For instance, according to research by Martin Gilens in his classic book *Why Americans Hate Welfare*, it was only after media imagery of the poor switched from mostly white to mostly black and brown (beginning in the early 1970s) that public anger about social spending began to explode. Prior to that time, most people understood the importance of safety nets, and they had been highly supportive of assistance to the poor from the period of the Great Depression well into the 1960s. But once the public came to view aid recipients as people of color, that support waned.

Likewise, Jill Quadagno points out in *The Color of Welfare* that the nation's most promising antipoverty initiatives and programs have been routinely undermined by racism aimed at those perceived to be the disproportionate beneficiaries. Indeed, racist opposition to the empowerment of blacks was among the principal reasons that President Nixon's proposal for a guaranteed minimum national income was rejected. Kenneth Neubeck and Noel Cazenave put forth a similar analysis in their book *Welfare Racism: Playing the Race Card Against America's Poor*. Neubeck and Cazenave document the way that politicians have used racial resentment and racism to limit public assistance of all kinds, and have been more focused on using welfare policy to control black and brown labor mobility and even reproduction, than on providing real opportunity and support. Again, the irony should be clear: because of the racialization of social policy, those of us who are struggling will now have less of a safety net to catch us than might otherwise have been the case.

In fact, a comprehensive comparison of various social programs in the United States and Europe found that racial hostility to people of color better explains opposition to high levels of social spending here than any other economic or political variable.

If we read our history carefully we can see how this process has played out. It used to be the case that most of us had sympathy for those who were poor and struggling. While the wealthy have long been given to questioning the character of the poor—think Ebeneezer Scrooge's famous soliloquy from Dickens's *A Christmas Carol*—such judgmentalism has not been the norm for average, everyday folks until relatively recently. For most of our history, we understood that people sometimes found themselves the victims of circumstances beyond their control. So in the 1930s, for instance, most of us understood that millions were poor and desperate not because there was something wrong with their character, their work ethic or their morals, but because of structural economic conditions like the stock market collapse or the Dust Bowl droughts in the Midwest. Thus we supported assistance to people in need. Even if we were managing to keep our heads above water, we saw those who were struggling as ourselves, or at least as metaphorical brothers and sisters about whom our concern was genuine.

Even in the 1980s, when thousands of farmers were losing their land to foreclosures, again in large part because of economic factors beyond their control, we believed in bailing them out. We saw the enemy in those cases as greedy banks, taking advantage of struggling farm families who were the backbone of America, and corporate farmers who were snapping up land and pushing family farms out of business to amass mega-profits. We did not, by and large, blame the small farmers for their station.

But when we speak of urban poverty and the conditions of life facing millions of low-income people of color, our rhetoric is quite different as is our level of compassion and forbearance. For them, character-ological judgment and condemnation is our first reflex. Whereas white folks are the innocent and deserving poor, black and brown folks are guilty (of something) and undeserving; their condition is believed by most of us to be the fault of their own pathologies and dysfunctions.

And this is not to say that those pathologies are never real. Of course they are. Intense poverty primes personal dysfunction in any society. Desperate and defeated peoples often fail to put their best foot forward. But the question is, which of these came first? We tend to give our own poor the benefit of the doubt—their pathological behaviors stem from the conditions to which they have been subjected, but deep down, they remain good people—while for persons of color, we presume that it was their pathology that caused their poverty, and so little compassion need attach. We become indifferent.

But the fate of the poor and working-class—disproportionately of color—is directly tied to the fate of the rest of us, however much we may have ignored that truth for years. Growing economic inequalities in America, which have long had a racial cast to them, are a key contributor to the nation's economic crisis and a principal reason it appears so hard to pull out of the mess. When vast numbers of people can no longer afford to purchase goods and services, those who make goods and offer services can't sell them either. So they cut back on production, which means they cut back on hiring, and choose instead to sit on massive reserves of cash. As of now, corporate America is hoarding over $2 trillion in cash reserves—and banks are hoarding trillions more—rather than creating new employment opportunities or lending out that money for the purposes of investment and production. Although we might as cribe such actions to simple greed, the larger truth is that unless average, everyday folks have the income to buy what those companies might otherwise produce, the companies themselves can't really do much else. While the negative demand-side effects of inequality could be finessed for a while thanks to building consumer debt all throughout the 1990s, as the credit crunch spreads and the borrowing bubble bursts, the phony promises of a credit-card economy have come crashing down around us.

Sadly, those of us who have fallen prey to the siren song of the right are lining up behind a political and economic agenda that offers no way out of this mess, and indeed would make it worse. Conservatives propose only to slash taxes on corporations and wealthy individuals, or to reduce regulations so as to ostensibly free up more potential investment dollars with which those companies and persons could create jobs. But if these folks are already flush with cash, what good will tax cuts do? How can such policies spur economic development, hiring and growth when incomes for most workers remain stagnant, and have been so for nearly *three decades*, thereby depressing demand? Corporate profitability is at its highest point in fifty years, and nearly 90 percent of the nation's recent income growth has gone to corporate profits (while only about one-tenth of one percent went to worker wages), suggesting that if all such entities needed was more money to restart the engine of employment, they would have done it long ago. If $2 trillion in cash reserves fails to spark a hiring spree, why would anyone assume that another $300 billion or so would make the difference? Rather, such tax cuts would simply reduce revenues for vital programs in education, health care and public sector job creation. They would result in the further evisceration of the safety net at the very moment when millions of people are increasingly in need of it.

Once again, none of this is merely an academic point. If we allow ourselves to become indifferent to the suffering of some, because we view them as responsible for their own plight or as bad people, then the programs and efforts we might otherwise have supported (and once did) for those in need will cease to exist as effective measures. Then, having allowed our biases to cloud our judgment and influence our public policy decisions, we will find ourselves—as we are now—without those very safety nets needed for our own support: their pain and our pain become one.

Meanwhile, having become inured to the suffering of others, we find that others become inured to *our* suffering, too, and look down on us just as we long looked down on others who were hurting, unemployed or poor. As millions of us face the prospects of long-term unemployment, the conservative politicians behind whom we have increasingly lined up offer nothing but condemnation and contempt. They suggest that if you're out of work it's because you aren't looking hard enough for a job, never mind that there are routinely dozens if not hundreds of people applying for each available job opening. They bash you for relying on unemployment insurance and insist that such "handouts" encourage sloth, even though the amount of the benefits (for which many unemployed people don't even qualify) are nowhere near sufficient to replace an actual salary. Presidential candidate and conservative stalwart, Newt Gingrich, for instance, has recently argued that there is something "inherently wrong" with paying people something for not working, as if to suggest that unemployed persons are to blame for having lost their jobs and that it would be more moral to force them into even greater desperation than to aid them, by cutting off unemployment benefits, so as to presumably teach them a lesson.

In that *Newsweek* cover story I mentioned earlier, back in spring 2011, concerning the job troubles facing even well-educated, white-collar white men, one of the former executives interviewed mentioned how shameful his current situation is, and how every time he's out looking for work he feels like he's got a neon sign around him that says "unemployed bum." But how did it come to this? And why? When did we decide that the unemployed, or those losing their homes, or those who were struggling were bums? Was that the operative mindset during the Great Depression? No. But it is today, and it is a mindset that is part and parcel of the Tea Party mentality that has infected so much of our community.

Remember, it was CNBC business reporter Rick Santelli who first conjured historical tea party imagery in opposition to government support for struggling homeowners. Santelli, who is still credited by Tea

Party activists as having issued the "rant heard 'round the world," and is very much seen as the godfather of the movement, aimed his vitriol not at Wall Street fat cats who had tanked the economy, not at lawmakers who had run up deficits to support wars for which they hadn't seen fit to pay, but rather at those he termed the "losers," who had gotten in over their heads with their mortgages. Standing on the floor of the commodities exchange in Chicago, Santelli bellowed about the injustice of bailing out people who had taken out loans they couldn't afford, ignoring the fact that lenders had preyed upon millions of borrowers with dishonest claims about their loans, or written loans with far higher rates of interest than what the borrowers should have qualified for. To Santelli, and the wealthy white male brokers with whom he communed as he issued the rant, the working-class and middle-class folks who were now following the poor off the economic cliff were to be scorned, rebuked, made the butt of a joke. They—and that means many of *you*—are losers to the business class, as represented by the likes of Santelli. The Tea Party movement was not born of concern over deficits, or taxes, or adherence to the strict wording of the Constitution. Rather, it was born of deep-seated contempt for the pain of average, everyday people. It was born of a temper tantrum thrown by a spoiled, rich white man, surrounded by other spoiled, rich white men who do not see those who struggle to pay their bills as their equals, as Americans worthy of concern or compassion. They view them as hardly human. The seeds of the Tea Party movement, in other words, were sown in the soil of cruelty. Are we not capable of better than that?

∞

But there is one more thing that helps explain the depths of the trauma that so many of us seem to be experiencing at present. And by trauma, I am speaking of the psychological blow of the great recession, rather than merely its financial impact.

A little over a year ago, I engaged in a rather lengthy and generally quite constructive email exchange with a man named Jeremy—white and unemployed at that time for twenty-six weeks—who was especially thrown off stride by the realization that although he had done "everything right" and "played by the rules" and "stayed in school" and "worked hard," he was still unable to find a job. That Jeremy felt a special kind of injury based on his having worked hard and played by the rules, yet still found himself in the position he was in, is worth exploring at length. This part of his story was, to me at least, especially telling, for it portended a sense on Jeremy's part that he deserved better than this and should have been able to expect better. People like him are not supposed to be out of work and struggling. Perhaps others are (those who haven't his work ethic, for instance), but not people like him.

What is so interesting about this narrative of expectation and entitlement is how contingent it was on Jeremy's race, whether or not he realized it, and whether or not most of us would see it as such. The fact is, people of color, no matter how hard they've worked, and no matter their level of education, have *never* been able to take for granted that their merit and initiative would pay off. They have never had the luxury of buying into the narrative of meritocracy the way we have, because they have seen family members, friends and others in their communities work hard every day and get nowhere fast. In this sense, the white mythology of America, which people of color have had no choice but to question and have always know to be only a partial truth on a good day, is one that has set up Jeremy and others like him. By convincing white men that all they had to do was work hard, that mythology—and white men's privilege of being able to buy into it, and their privilege of having it work most of the time—has let them down doubly hard. It's one thing to suffer. But to suffer when you were told by the culture that suffering was not, by and large, the lot of people like you, is to experience a psychic blow that is magnified tenfold.

When one's illusions are shattered, it is never a

pretty thing. To come to realize that everything we assumed about our society was a lie is nothing if not discomfiting. That people of color almost always saw things for what they were points out another irony of the current moment: the fact that the folks being hit hardest by the downturn (who are indeed still people of color) are perhaps the most prepared to deal with it, cope and survive; meanwhile, those who had been able to count on the system more or less working for them may be the ones least prepared to do so.

It brings to mind the Great Depression, during which it was never the poor or folks of color who went to the tops of buildings and threw themselves off, unable to face the prospects of financial ruin. Rather, it was the white and wealthy who saw a bump in suicide rates, so unprepared were they to deal with setback. Likewise, consider the way that adult children of parents who decide to divorce after forty years of marriage so often take the news harder than even the pre-teen whose parents do the same. The pre-teen has had nowhere near enough time to construct a mythologized image of his or her parents, or their love for one another. But when you have grown up assuming the sanguinity of the home in which you were raised, only to learn that perhaps things were not as they seemed, it can seem as if the whole world is collapsing.

This, it appears, is where many of us find ourselves now: unmoored, untethered, adrift on a sea of shattered illusions. Interestingly, had the society been less committed to the myth than to creating a reality of equity and opportunity for all, perhaps what Jeremy and millions of us are experiencing right now would never have come to pass. Had the culture not set white men up to expect the world, precisely because they were deemed superior to everyone else, the mental anguish and esteem-battering currently under way could have been prevented. Perhaps if we had been serious about making the deed match the word, and had we encouraged the kind of unity needed to make a society livable for all, things would have been different. If we had understood our job to be the achievement of our national promise as a real and living thing, rather than merely the recitation of a handful of platitudes, devoid of animation, much pain could have been circumvented altogether.

One thing is certain: we will have to allow ourselves to wake up now to the harsh realities that we have been so assiduously encouraged to ignore. For a long time, and for most of us, life was a matter of simply following the directions on a roadmap, confident that if we paid close enough attention and followed them religiously, we'd likely end up at our preferred destination. Play by the rules, work hard, study hard, plan for the future and put away some reserve monies for a rainy day. But the truth is, we never believed in rainy days, I mean never *really* believed in them, and never *this* much rain. People of color knew the weather, made sure in fact never to leave home without at least a metaphorical umbrella close at hand, but we didn't. Rain was what happened to others, but not to us. Or if it did touch us, it was but a temporary shower, just sufficient to remind us to stay on our toes, but never enough of a downpour to make us question the larger forecast we'd been given by the meteorologists of our culture.

Now, as the economy implodes and the future creeps up on us as thick and murky as chowder, those directions we've been following seem no longer to suffice. They are akin to the instructions barked out at us from a GPS device sitting atop our dashboard, but which, sadly, were programmed long ago, before the terrain had changed. So now we're doing as the stern voice suggests we should, but we're finding ourselves lost, realizing that the turn she told us to take hasn't brought us to the place we thought it would. There are new roads, new subdivisions in the society we thought we knew, detours that hadn't existed before, dead ends that now choke off the path that just a few years earlier seemed so simple and straightforward.

Of course, our first inclination when led astray by an outdated GPS is to curse the machine, forgetting that it was programmed by fallible people just like us, who thought they knew every twist and turn but had actually missed the changes about which we would have done well to know. At some point, we realize, and hopefully not too late, that we have to look inward and question our reliance on the machine in the first place. The GPS does what the GPS was made to do. It has no brain separate and apart from those of the men and women who built it. It will pick the route and instruct us to take it, and even if it manages to give us multiple choices—the shortest path or perhaps the one with the least traffic or the one that is the most scenic—it can only do this because some flesh-and-blood human being told the machine which options existed, which is to say, the machine is merely selecting from a pre-prepared set of possibilities provided by a person whose own horizons may well have been limited. The machine cannot, literally, choose.

But we had a choice. We have one now. And that choice is whether we are going to continue to rely uncritically on an outdated set of directions, barked at us by a machine of our own making, or perhaps question those directions, perhaps create a new set of instructions for how to thrive and arrive at that destination of personal and collective accomplishment we euphemistically call the "good life." Perhaps we can fashion a set of collective goals that will move us toward the place we were meant to be, toward the promise that has always been this nation, however unfulfilled and half empty the promise has long been.

I know this much: if we, white America, do not quickly relinquish the remaining grip exercised by the national mythology, it will continue to batter us, to insult us, to mock our hard work and suffering, and to reinforce the self-loathing that has been its primary product for generations. And it will render our nation utterly unworkable in years to come. How, after all, can the United States remain an economically viable nation if we get to that place thirty years from now where people of color are half of the population, and yet still twice as likely as whites to be unemployed and three times as likely to be poor? How can we remain an even remotely productive and functioning society when half of our population has nine years' less life expectancy, double the rate of infant mortality and children born with low birth weight, and one-twentieth the net worth, on average, as the other half? The answer is that we cannot, and will not. Equity is the last, and only, remaining hope for this experiment we call the United States.

∞

The good news is that we *can* change. Redemption, both for us as white folks and for the nation as a whole, is possible. In fact, the path for that change has already been laid out before us, long ago and for many generations, by some within our own group, following the lead of people of color and working in solidarity with them to build a better and more just society. However much we may have been unaware of this path, it is incumbent upon us to discover it, or rediscover it, now.

Imagine how different the racial dialogue might feel for us if we knew and had been taught from a young age of the history of white allyship and antiracist resistance? If as children we had been introduced not only to the black and brown heroes and sheroes of the antiracist struggle—like Frederick Douglass, Sojourner Truth, Rosa Parks, Fannie Lou Hamer, Ella Baker and of course Dr. King—but also to those white freedom fighters who stood beside them? What if we learned of the alternative tradition in our history, the one in which members of *our* community said no to racism and white domination, said no to unearned privilege and inequality, said no to racial hegemony and *yes* to justice?

What if we had learned of those persons of European descent who stood with their African counterparts during Bacon's Rebellion, recognizing that they had far more in common with most blacks than with the white elite for whom they toiled? What if we had learned of those whites who opposed enslavement and segregation precisely because they realized not only the moral evil of such systems, but also because they saw both as cynical manipulations intended to divide and conquer working people, to keep them at each others' throats while the rich and powerful continued to hoard the wealth that they, the workers, had created?

The fact is, we know almost nothing of that alternative tradition at present. In addition to the typically pathetic and piecemeal way our history books address the contributions of people of color, even the whites we learn about are from a narrow and cramped range of human experience: founding fathers, military heroes and wealthy industrialists. Rarely is much attention paid to the average, everyday whites who stood in opposition to the actions of so many of the leaders in our own community, and when such persons are discussed it is usually only within the context of the martyrdom that many attained, killed for their efforts to destroy slavery or segregation. But for each one who died, more still survived to tell the story and continue the struggle. What if we knew about *them*?

In this moment of white anxiety and profound social change—in which our normalcy and *a priori* claim on Americanness can no longer be taken for granted—how helpful might it be (in terms of lessening our anxiety and allowing us to embrace the multiracial and multicultural future) if we knew about the history of white antiracism, multiracial solidarity and allyship? How much less stressful might the current moment of societal transformation be, if we knew the names and stories of Jeremiah Evarts, William Shreve Bailey, John Fee, Helen Hunt Jackson, Sarah and Angelina Grimké, Robert Flournoy, George Henry Evans, Matilda Gage, Catherine Weldon, Lydia Child, Anne Braden, Will Campbell, Virginia Foster Durr, J. Waties Waring, Constance Curry, Bob and Dottie Zellner and Mab Segrest, along with literally thousands of others, who in their own way and in their own communities have demonstrated that there was more than one way to live in this skin? People who have demonstrated that the human values of equity, fairness and justice are not merely modern contrivances but rather timeless guide-posts that have historically been betrayed, bringing dishonor to our nation. Their stories call upon us now to do better. It strikes me as almost self-evident that were we to know of their stories, to embrace them as examples for our own lives, to model our commitments after theirs, to rally to the kind of nationhood that *they* envisioned, much about our current troubles would be different. We would perhaps begin to imagine a different world, in which the divisions of color that have so long roiled us would be the stuff of history, rather than current events.

And no, I won't tell the stories of the people whose

names I've rattled off above. Some homework has to be done alone. For starters, all should read Herbert Aptheker's majestic history of white antiracism from the colonial period to the civil war, *Anti-Racism in U.S. History: The First Two Hundred Years*. From there, we can discover or deepen our understanding of the proud tradition of white allyship during the civil rights struggle, chronicled in dozens of books and documentaries. This tradition I speak of is ours to claim, ours to follow, ours to emulate. If we let it, the tradition can inspire us, motivate us, transform us and transform the society in which we live. It is a tradition that fits with the best of the American ideal, and one that is capable of elevating that ideal to a place more stable and concrete than it has been heretofore.

Or, alternately, we can continue unimpeded on the current path of uncertainty, anxiety, resentment and trepidation. We can continue to hold on to a fictional, nostalgic past, longing for a return to it, and unable to embrace the changes that are as inevitable as the coming of the new day's sun. We can jealously seek to hold on to our current advantages, be they material or merely psychological—our own sense of betterness, belonging, or perhaps superior character—and squander the opportunity to grow, individually and collectively, into the full members of a democratic polity that we were meant to be.

One thing is certain though, we cannot hold onto the old ways and move into the future at the same time. Something in this equation will have to give. As James Baldwin once explained, many years ago, but even then anticipating this moment:

Any real change implies the breakup of the world as one has always known it, the loss of all that gave one an identity, the end of safety. And at such a moment, unable to see and not daring to imagine what the future will now bring forth, one clings to what one knew, or dreamed that one possessed. Yet, it is only when a man is able, without bitterness or self-pity, to surrender a dream he has long cherished or a privilege he has long possessed that he is set free—he has set himself free for higher dreams, for greater privileges.

Notes

Page 21

". . . the headright system . . . provided fifty acres of land": Information on the headright system can be found at http://en.wikipedia.org/wiki/Headright

"The Naturalization Act of 1790": Information on this law can be found at http://en.wikipedia.org/wiki/Naturalization_Act_of_1790

Page 26–27

Data on wealth and asset gaps between whites, blacks and Latinos is from Shawna Orzechowski and Peter Sepielli, *Net Worth and Asset Ownership of Households: 1998 and 2000*. Current Population Reports, pp. 70–88. (United States Bureau of the Census, Washington, DC, May 2003), pp. 2, 13–15.

Page 27

Data on widening racial wealth gaps, and the $100,000 difference in net worth between the typical white family and the typical black or Latino family comes from Ben Rooney, "Recession Widens Racial Gap," *CNN Money* (July 26, 2011), http://money.cnn.com/2011/07/26/news/economy/wealth_gap_white_black_hispanic/index.htm

". . . these financial wizards . . . lost over twelve trillion dollars of other people's money thanks to the shady practices that tanked the stock market" is from "Rep. Alan Grayson: $12 Trillion Gone and Nobody Punished," *DailyKos* (Feb. 13, 2010), www.dailykos.com/story/2010/02/13/836676/-Rep-Alan-Grayson:-$12-trillion-Gone-and-Nobody-Punished

Page 29–31

Data on the value of property stolen each year through traditional crime comes from FBI figures discussed at "Cost of Crime"

(National Center for Victims of Crime), www.ncvc.org/ncvc/main.
aspx?dbName=DocumentViewer&DocumentID=38710#_ftn4

The study that found more than 1.2 million cases of racial discrimination is Alfred Blumrosen and Ruth Blumrosen, *The Reality of Intentional Job Discrimination in Metropolitan America, 1999* (New Jersey: Rutgers University, 1999), www.eeo1.com_NR/Title.pdf

". . . lighter skinned immigrants, mostly from European nations, earn around 15 percent more than darker skinned immigrants, even when all their respective qualifications and markers of personal productivity are the same" is from "Study Says Light-Skinned Immigrants in U.S. Make More Money Than Darker-Skinned Ones," *Fox News.com* (January 27, 2007), www.foxnews.com/story/0,2933,247302,00.html, and Richard Morin, "Immigrants and the Whiter-Shade-of-Pale Bonus," *Washington Post.com* (October 18, 2006), www.washingtonpost.com/wp-dyn/content/article/2006/10/17/AR2006101701257.html

". . . even when a black person has a college degree, he or she is nearly twice as likely as one of us with a degree to be unemployed, while Latinos and Asian Americans with degrees are 40 percent more likely than we are to be out of work, with the same qualifications" is from the U.S. Department of Labor, 2009 *Labor Force Characteristics by Race and Ethnicity,* www.bls.gov/cps/cpsrace2009.pdf. Table 4. Because this table does not break out non-Hispanic whites from the white totals, it tends to inflate the unemployment rate for white workers, who are not also members of an ethnic "group of color." In Labor Department data, roughly 92 percent of Hispanics are counted in the "white" racial category and need to be removed in order to provide a "real" white unemployment rate. Once the figures in this table are adjusted, the "real" white unemployment rate falls to 4.1 percent. The black rate, by comparison, at 7.3 percent, is about 80 percent higher. The Asian American rate of 5.6 percent is about 37 percent higher than this white rate, and the Hispanic rate of 5.7 percent is about 39 percent higher than the white rate. As this volume was going to press, newer data from the Labor Department was released, available at www.bls.gov/cps/cpsrace2010.pdf. For 2010, this data indicates a "real white" unemployment rate of 4.15 percent. The black rate of 7.9 percent is about 90 percent higher than the white rate. The Asian American rate of 5.5 percent is approximately a third higher than this white rate, and the Hispanic rate of 6 percent is about 45 percent higher than this white rate.

". . . even when comparing only persons working in management, business and financial job categories, those of us in such occupations typically earn about 30 percent more in weekly income than our counterparts of color, amounting to nearly $13,000 in additional earnings each year, relative to African Americans and Latinos" is also from *Labor Force Characteristics by Race and Ethnicity*; see preceding note, www.bls.gov/cps/cpsrace2009.pdf, at Table 16, p. 44.

". . . median income for white men who are between twenty-five and thirty-four years old (early on in their careers) is one-third higher than the median for black men who are fifty-five to sixty-four years old and already nearing retirement" is from U.S. Census Bureau, Current Population Survey, *Annual Social and Economic Supplements*, www.census.gov/hhes/www/income/data/historical/people/index.html

". . . a white man with a criminal record is more likely to be called back for a job interview than a black man without one, even when their credentials are the same" is from Devah Pager and Bruce Western, *Race at Work: Realities of Race and Criminal Record in the NYC Job Market*, paper presented at the NYC Commission on Human Rights conference, Schomburg Center for Research in Black Culture (December 9, 2005), and Devah Pager, *Marked: Race, Crime and Finding Work in an Era of Mass Incarceration* (Chicago: University of Chicago Press, 2007), www.princeton.edu/~pager/race_at_work.pdf

Page 31
". . . millions of cases of race-based housing discrimination occurring each year" is from Douglass S. Massey and Nancy A. Denton,

American Apartheid: Segregation and the Making of the Underclass (Cambridge: Harvard University Press, 1993), 200; Deborah L. McKoy and Jeffrey M. Vincent, "Housing and Education: the Inextricable Link," in *Segregation: The Rising Costs for America*, James H. Carr and Nandinee K. Kutty, eds. (New York: Routledge, 2008), 128.

". . . when blacks have better credit, higher incomes, more reserve savings and less debt than we do, they are subjected to higher interest rates and generally treated worse by lenders in six out of ten instances" is from Sam Spatter, "Fair Housing Partnership Study: Blacks Still Face Mortgage Bias," *Pittsburgh Tribune Review* (November 25, 2009), www.pittsburghlive.com/x/pittsburghtrib/business/s_654803.html

Page 32

". . . even high-income African Americans were more likely than low-income whites to end up with a high-cost, subprime loan, and up to half of the subprime loans were given to persons who should have qualified for lower rates (and mostly would have, had they been white)" is from Applied Research Center, *Race and Recession: How Inequity Rigged the Economy and How to Change the Rules* (Oakland: Applied Research Center, May 2009), 37–39; Kathleen C. Engel and Patricia A. McCoy, "The CRA Implications of Predatory Lending," 29 *Fordham Urban Law Journal* 4 (2002), 1571–1606.

". . . schools that serve mostly African American students have twice as many teachers with only a year or two of experience as schools that serve white students, even when those schools are in the same districts" is from "New Data from the U.S. Department of Education, 2009-2010 Civil Rights Data Collection Show Continuing Disparities in Educational Opportunities and Resources" (U.S. Department of Education, press release, June 30, 2011), www.ed.gov/news/press-releases/new-data-us-department-education-2009-10-civil-rights-data-collection-show-conti

". . . new teachers in majority-minority schools are five times as likely as new teachers in mostly white schools to be uncertified

158

in the subject matter they are currently being asked to teach" is from Linda Darling-Hammond, "Unequal Opportunity: Race and Education," *Brookings Review*. Spring, 1998: 31.

Page 33

". . . within given schools, the least experienced and least effective teachers are regularly matched with the most challenging students . . . (who are often low-income students of color in need of highly capable instruction), while the most experienced and effective teachers are paired with white, high achieving students" is from Demetra Kalogrides, Susanna Loeb and Tara Béteille, *Power Play? Teacher Characteristics and Class Assignments* (Urban Institute, National Center for Analysis of Longitudinal data in Education Research, Working Paper 59, March 2011)

". . . schools that serve mostly black and Latino students are also more than ten times as likely as the schools most of our kids attend to be places of concentrated poverty" is from Gary Orfield et al., "Deepening Segregation in American Public Schools: A Special Report From the Harvard Project on School Desegregation," *Equity & Excellence in Education*, 30, 1997, 5–24; Valerie Martinez-Ebers, "Latino Interests in Education, Health and Criminal Justice Policy," *Political Science and Politics* (September 2000);

". . . and are far less likely to offer a full complement of advanced classes" is from Daniel G. Solorzano and Armida Ornelas, "A Critical Race Analysis of Latina/o and African American Advanced Placement Enrollment in Public High Schools," *The High School Journal* (Vol. 87: 3, February-March 2004), www.jstor.org/pss/40364293; Philip Handwerk, Namrata Tognatta, Richard J. Coley, and Drew H. Gitomer, *Access to Success: Patterns of Advanced Placement Participation in U.S. High Schools* (Princeton, N.J., Educational Testing Service, 2008), www.ets.org/Media/Research/pdf/PIC-ACCESS.pdf

Page 33–34

". . . schools with mostly white students typically receive more money per pupil for direct instruction than schools serving mostly students of color" is from   Raegen Miller and Diana Epstein, "There Still be Dragons: Racial Disparity in School Funding Is No Myth," (Center for American Progress, July 2011), www. americanprogress.org/issues/2011/07/still_be_dragons.html; Kevin Carey, *The Funding Gap: Low Income and Minority Students Still Receive Fewer Dollars in Many States* (Washington DC, The Education Trust, 2003).

Page 34
". . . in 1964, about two-thirds of all persons incarcerated in this country were white, while one-third were persons of color. By the mid-1990s, those numbers had reversed, so that now, two-thirds of persons locked up are black and brown, while only a third are white" is from *World Without Work: Causes and Consequences of Black Male Joblessness* (Center for the Study of Social Policy and the Philadelphia Children's Network, 1994); Paige Harrison and Jennifer Karberg, *Prison and Jail Inmates at Midyear 2002* (U.S. Department of Justice, Bureau of Justice Statistics, Bulletin, April 2003).

Page 35
". . . whites comprise roughly 70 percent of all drug users and are every bit as likely as people of color to use drugs" is a calculation that can be made from the data in, Substance Abuse and Mental Health Services Administration (SAMHSA), *Results from the 2009 National Survey on Drug Use and Health: Volume I. Summary of National Findings*. (Office of Applied Studies, NSDUH Series H-38A, HHS Publication No. SMA10-4586, Rockville, MD., 2010), as well as all similar years of SAMHSA data dating back to the 1990s. In some years, white drug usage rates are slightly higher that the rates for persons of color, while in others, the rates for persons of color are higher. At other times, the rates of use are similar, within the range of statistically insignificant differences. When the data are longitudinally examined over a decade or so, there is little argument that whites, blacks and Latinos use drugs are comparable rates; also see data from Human Rights Watch, at www.hrw.org/reports/2009/03/02/decades-disparity-0,   www.hrw. org/en/reports/2008/05/04/targeting-blacks

". . . nine in ten people locked up each year for a possession offense are people of color" is from Jim Sidanius, Shana Levin and Felicia Pratto, "Hierarchial Group Relations, Institutional Terror and the Dynamics of the Criminal Justice System," in *Confronting Racism: The Problem and the Response*, Jennifer Eberhardt and Susan T. Fiske, eds. (London: Sage Publications, 1998).

"Black youth are nearly fifty times as likely as our youth to be incarcerated for a first-time drug offense, even when all the factors surrounding the crime (like whether or not a weapon was involved) are equal" is from Eileen Poe-Yamagata and Michael A. Jones, *And Justice for Some: Differential Treatment of Minority Youth in the Justice System* (Washington, DC: Building Blocks for Youth, 2000).

"Even though they are less likely than we are to be found with drugs or other illegal contraband when searched by police, blacks and Latinos are far more likely than we are to be stopped and searched by law enforcement looking for such items" is from Matthew R. Durose, Erica L. Schmitt and Patrick A. Langan, *Contacts Between Police and the Public: Findings from the 2002 National Survey* (U.S. Department of Justice, Bureau of Justice Statistics, April 2005), http://bjs.ojp.usdoj.gov/content/pub/pdf/cpp02.pdf

Page 36
". . . (in the early 1960s) . . . two-thirds of us said blacks had equal opportunity in employment, education and housing," and "In one 1962 survey, roughly 90 percent of us said that we believed black children had just as good a chance to get a quality education as we or our children did," both from The Gallup Organization, Gallup Poll Social Audit, *Black-White Relations in the United States, 2001 Update* (July 10, 2001), pp. 7–9.

Page 42
"Across virtually all job and educational attainment levels, blacks and Latinos with the same levels of education, working in the same occupations, routinely have double the rates of unemployment experienced by whites" is from *Labor Force Characteristics by Race and Ethnicity, 2010* (United States Department of Labor: Bureau

of Labor Statistics, Report 1032, August, 2011), www.bls.gov/cps/cpsrace2010.pdf

Page 43

"African American children from middle-class and affluent households are also far more likely than their white counterparts to attend high-poverty schools" is from Massey and Denton, 1993 (previously cited: see page 31), pp. 86, 153.

". . . to be relegated to low-track classes" is from Jeannie Oakes, "Two cities' tracking and within-school segregation," *Teachers College Record*, 96(4), 1995: pp. 681–690.

". . . to be suspended or expelled from school altogether, despite breaking serious school rules no more often than white students from the same socioeconomic status" is from Russell Skiba et al., *The Color of Discipline: Sources of Racial and Gender Disproportionality in School Punishment* (Indiana Education Policy Center, Research Report SRS1, June 2000); and the same authors in *The Urban Review* 34(4) (December 2002), www.springerlink.com/content/m1u480614844118x/

". . . are subjected, according to the available evidence, to racial profiling of all types" is from Joe Feagin and Melvin Sikes, *Living With Racism: The Black Middle Class Experience* (Boston: Beacon Press, 1995); Annie Barnes, *Say it Loud: Middle Class Blacks Talk About Racism and What to Do About It* (Pilgrim Press, 2000).

Page 44

"According to one study from the 1990s—at which point the out-of-wedlock birth rates in the black community had already climbed to their current high levels—even if these rates had remained the same since the 1960s and not budged upward at all, nearly all the income and poverty-rate gaps between whites and blacks would have remained the same" is from Michael K. Brown, Martin Carnoy, Elliott Currie, Troy Duster, David B. Oppenheimer, Marjorie M. Shultz and David Wellman, *Whitewashing Race: The Myth of a Color-Blind Society* (Berkeley: University of California Press, 2003), p. 89.

". . . black married couples are twice as likely as their white counterparts to be poor, and Latino married couples are more than four times as likely as married whites to be poor" is from United States Department of Commerce, Bureau of the Census, "Poverty in the United States, 2000," *Current Population Survey* (March 2000).

". . . nearly one in five black children growing up in a two-parent home lives in poverty, more than double the rate for white children, while one in four Latino/a kids in a two-parent home remains poor—roughly equal to the rate at which white children in single-mother families experience poverty" is from Rose M. Kreider and Renee Ellis, *Living Arrangements of Children: 2009*. Current Population Reports, P70-126 (United States Bureau of the Census, Washington, DC, 2011), Table 8, p. 20.

". . . when black and Latina women are single moms, they are nearly twice as likely as our single moms to be poor" is from Carmen Denavas-Walt, Bernadette D. Proctor and Jessica C. Smith, *Income, Poverty and Health Insurance Coverage in the United States: 2009*, Current Population Reports, pp. 60–238 (U.S. Bureau of the Census, Washington, DC, 2010), Table B1, pp. 58, 61, available at: www.census.gov/prod/2010pubs/p60-238.pdf

Page 45
". . . birth rates for black women under the age of eighteen (almost all of them unmarried) have fallen by more than a third since the early 1990s" is from Centers for Disease Control and Prevention, *National Vital Statistics Reports* 49:10 (September 25, 2001): pp. 1–4, 11, Table 2; also Joyce A. Martin, Brady E. Hamilton, Paul D. Sutton, Stephanie J. Ventura, T.J. Mathews, Sharon Kirmeyer and Michelle J.K. Osterman, "Births: Final Data for 2007," *National Vital Statistics Reports* 58: 24 (August 9, 2010), www.cdc.gov/nchs/data/nvsr/nvsr58/nvsr58_24.pdf

". . . fertility rates among all unmarried black women have plummeted since the 1970s" is from Steven A. Holmes, "Black Birthrate for Single Women Is at 40-Year Low," *New York Times*, July 1, 1998: A1.

That the rise in out-of-wedlock births in the black community is due to the large drop in the number of children being born to two-parent black couples, as opposed to an explosion among single black women, is from Lucy Williams, *Decades of Distortion: The Right's 30-Year Assault on Welfare* (Somerville, MA: Political Research Associates, December 1997), p. 2.

Pages 45–46
Information on how few people of color actually receive various forms of "welfare" provision is from Tracy Loveless and Jan Tin, *Dynamics of Economic Well-Being: Participation in Government Programs, 2001 Through 2003 Who Gets Assistance?"* Current Population Reports, P70-108 (United States Bureau of the Census, Household Economic Studies, October 2006), Tables A-2, A-4 and A-6, pp. 18, 20, 22.

Page 46
". . . the median monthly value of cash and food assistance combined comes to only $255 per person": Loveless and Tin, 2006 (previously cited: see pages 45–46), Table A-8, p. 25.

". . . nearly eight in ten [welfare recipients] are either already working, looking regularly for work but unable to find a job, in school, or unable to work because of a persistent health condition" is from Shelley Irving, "TANF Participation and Employment in SIPP, 2004–2007," for presentation at the 2010 Annual Meeting of the American Sociological Association, August 14, 2010.

Pages 46–47
That there are not enough jobs available for those seeking work: Joshua Holland, "8 Unemployed for Every Job Opening: What are They Supposed to Do Once Their Benefits Run Out?" *Alternet. org* (March 23, 2011), www.alternet.org/economy/150358/8_ unemployed_for_every_job_opening%3A_what_are_they_ supposed_to_do_once_their_benefits_run_out/

". . . McDonalds recently held a massive national employee search, in which they were only able to hire six out of every hundred applicants" is from Scott Paul, "Shocker: Only 6 Out of 100

Applicants Can Get a Job at McDonalds It's Time for Politicians to Stop Ignoring Our Jobs Crisis," *Alternet.org* (May 4, 2011), www.alternet.org/story/150839/shocker%3A_only_6_out_of_100_applicants_can_get_a_job_at_mcdonald%27s_--_it%27s_time_for_politicians_to_stop_ignoring_our_jobs_crisis/

Page 47
Information on the median duration for receipt of various "welfare" benefits: Loveless and Tin, 2006, (previously cited: see pages 45–46), Table A-7

Page 48
"One study that looked at 40,000 students in grades seven through eleven actually found that it was white males—in other words, many of us and our children—who were the least likely of any group to say that good grades were 'very important' to them" is from Sarah Carr, "Coalition Says Study Rebuts Education Myths: Responses Demonstrate Commitment of Minority Students, Educators Say," *Milwaukee Journal Sentinel Online* (November 19, 2002), www.jsonline.com/news/metro/nov02/97244; Catherine Gewertz, "No Racial Gap Seen in Students' School Outlook," *Education Week* (November 20, 2002).

Pages 48–49
"Another study, which examined measures of academic honesty and integrity among students in different racial and ethnic groups, found that it was we and our children who were more likely than kids of color to believe it was acceptable to cheat, cut class or talk back to teachers. In fact, the group that had the lowest measures of academic integrity were affluent whites" is from Judith Blau, *Race in the Schools: Perpetuating White Dominance?* (Lynne Rienner Publishers, 2003): pp. 57–59, 84–85, 92–93.

Page 50
". . . they provided as much as $1 trillion in unpaid labor under the system of enslavement" is from Charles P. Henry, *Long Overdue: The Politics of Racial Reparation* (New York University Press, 2007), p. 171.

That blacks are three times as likely as whites to be poor is from DeNavas-Walt, Proctor and Smith, 2010 (previously cited: see page 44), Table 4, p. 15.

Page 51
". . . 100,000 black folks die annually who wouldn't if their mortality rates were level with those of whites" is from Adam Serwer, "The De-Facto Segregation of Health Care," *American Prospect* (August 21, 2009), http://prospect.org/cs/articles?article=the_defacto_ segregation_of_health_care; Ryan Blitstein, "Racism's Hidden Toll," *Miller-McCune* (June 2009), http://miller-mccune.com/ health/racisms-hidden-toll-1268?article_page=1

". . . African American households today have median incomes that are one-third lower, adjusted for inflation, than what white households were bringing in forty years ago" is from Denavas-Walt, Proctor and Smith, 2010 (previously cited: see page 44), Table A-1, pp. 35–36, referenced above, www.census.gov/prod/2010pubs/ p60-238.pdf

Pages 51–52
Information on measures of white versus black work ethic is from Rebecca Perron, *African American Experiences in the Economy: Recession Effects More Strongly Felt* (American Association for Retired Persons, February 2010); and William Julius Wilson, *More Than Just Race: Being Black and Poor in the Inner City* (NY: W. W. Norton and Company, 2010)

Page 52
". . . whites are three times as likely as similar African Americans to say that the reason they aren't working is because they are "not interested" in having a job, while blacks who are not working are 2.5 times as likely to be out of work because they can't find work" is from Nasrin Dalirizar, *Reasons People do Not Work: 2004*. P70-111 (United States Bureau of the Census, Washington, DC, 2007).

Pages 52–53

Information on white ethnic immigrants and how they received opportunities off-limits to native-born people of color in the United States is from Matthew Frye Jacobsen, *Whiteness of a Different Color: European Immigrants and the Alchemy of Race* (Cambridge: Harvard University Press, 1999); Noel Ignatiev, *How the Irish Became White* (NY: Routledge, 2008).

Page 53

Information on violence and anti-black race riots aimed at African Americans moving North is from Massey and Denton, 1993 (previously cited: see page 31).

Pages 54

That Asian Americans largely arrive in the U.S. with pre-existing educational and occupational advantages is from Stephen Steinberg, *The Ethnic Myth* (Boston: Beacon Press, 1989); Fox Butterfield, "Why Asians Are Going to the Head of the Class," *New York Times* (education supplement), August 3, 1986; Gary Mar, "Are Asians Model Minorities?" (2001), http://academic.udayton. edu/race/01race/model01.htm; U.S. Federal Glass Ceiling Commission, *Good for Business: Making Full Use of the Nation's Human Capital* (Washington, DC: Bureau of National Affairs, March 1995), p. 107; Vijay Prashad, *The Karma of Brown Folk* (Minneapolis, MN: University of Minnesota Press, 2000), p. 75.

Pages 54

Information on Asian American poverty rates and comparisons with white poverty rates is Census data, found at: www.asian-nation.org/demographics.shtml

Page 55

That Asian Americans are concentrated in a handful of relatively high-income and high-cost places, geographically, is from www. asian-nation.org/population.shtml; and Terrance Reeves and Claudette Bennett, "The Asian and pacific Islander Population in the United States: March 2002," *Current Population Reports*, pp. 20–540 (Washington, DC: U.S. Bureau of the Census, May 2003).

That Asian poverty rates are often twice the rate for whites in the same locale, is from Nancy Rivera Brooks, "Study Attacks Belief in Asian American Affluence, Privilege," *San Jose Mercury News* (May 19, 1994), 1A; Rosalind S. Chou and Joe R. Feagin, *The Myth of the Model Minority: Asian Americans Facing Racism* (Boulder, CO: Paradigm Publishers, 2008), p. 12.

That Asians earn less than whites at most all educational attainment levels, is from *A Snapshot of 'A Portrait of Chinese Americans,' Key Findings* (Washington, DC, and College Park, MD.: Organization of Chinese Americans and the Asian American Studies Program, University of Maryland, November 2008), p. 5.

"Chinese Americans in professional occupations (who are a highly educated group), earn only 56 percent as much as their white counterparts" is from "Major Study of Asian Americans Debunks 'Model Minority' Myth," *Science Daily* (November 12, 2008), www. sciencedaily.com/releases/2008/11/081112101339.htm

Pages 55–56
". . . the only reason that Asian household income tops that for whites, on average, is because Asian households tend to be larger and have more income earners per household than our households" is from Reeves and Bennett, 2003 (previously cited: see page 54), p. 3.

". . . per capita income remains lower for Asian Americans than for whites" is from DeNavas-Walt, Proctor and Smith, 2010 (previously cited: see page 44), Table 1, p. 6.

Page 57
Information on awareness of negative stereotypes by youth of color at an early age is from Clark McKown and Michael Strambler, "Developmental Antecedents and Social and Academic Consequences of Stereotype-Consciousness in Middle Childhood," *Child Development* 80(6) (November 2009), pp. 1643–1659.

Page 63

That most whites, even in many blue states, voted against Barack Obama in 2008 is from exit poll data compiled by CNN at www. cnn.com/ELECTION/2008/results/polls/#USP00p1

That white voter turnout was down by 700,000 in 2008 is from Mike Davis, "Obama at Manassas," *New Left Review* (March-April 2009), p. 24.

Page 64

For evidence of racist signage brought to anti-Obama rallies from 2008-2010, or racist e-mails sent by conservative activists, see http://images.huffingtonpost.com/gadgets/slideshows/1398/ slide_1398_20072_large.jpg; http://i2.cdn.turner.com/cnn/2009/ POLITICS/09/17/obama.witchdoctor.teaparty/art.obama. protest.sign.cnn.jpg; http://firedoglake.com/2010/03/07/ doesnt-it-seem-like-every-week-some-republican-asshole-gets-caught-sending-a-racist-email/; www.fitsnews.com/2009/06/12/ scgop-activist-posts-remark-disparaging-first-lady/; www. nashvillescene.com/pitw/archives/2009/06/15/republican-staffer-e-mails-obama-spook-photo; http://tpmmuckraker. talkingpointsmemo.com/2009/07/conservative_activist_forwards_ racist_pic_showing.php; www.huffingtonpost.com/2009/02/25/ white-house-watermelon-em_n_169933.html; www.flickr.com/ photos/jr1882/3792322329/; http://twitpic.com/hhll6i; www. examiner.com/liberal-in-anchorage/video-9-12-teabaggers-flaunt-racism-ignorance; http://crooksandliars.com/john-amato/ dr-david-mckalip-mr-tea-party-forwards; www.oliverwillis. com/2009/08/04/racism-on-display-in-anti-health-care-rallies/; http://colorlines.com/archives/2011/04/gop_member_sends_ email_depicting_obama_family_as_apes.html

That the 2010 GOP gubernatorial candidate in New York sent around racist e-mails is from Zachary Roth, "Tea Party New York Gov's Candidate's E-Mails Exposed: Racism, Porn, Bestiality," *Talking Points Memo.com* (April 12, 2010), http://tpmmuckraker. talkingpointsmemo.com/2010/04/tea_party_gov_candidates_ racist_sexually_graphic_e.php

That Glenn Beck claimed the president's health care reform package was just a form of "reparations" for slavery is from "Glenn Beck: Obama agenda driven by 'reparations' and desire to 'settle old racial scores,'" *Media Matters.org* (July 23, 2009), http://mediamatters.org/mmtv/200907230040

"Rush Limbaugh . . . claimed that the president is deliberately trying to destroy the economy and 'happily' presiding 'over the decline of America' as 'payback' for the history of racism and slavery" is from Laura Bassett, "Rush Limbaugh: Obama Created Recession as 'Payback' for Racism," *Huffington Post.com* (July 7, 2010), www.huffingtonpost.com/2010/07/07/rush-limbaugh-obama-creat_n_637716.html

Page 65
That Eric Bolling accused President Obama of hosting "hoodlums in the hizzouse" is from "Fox's Eric Bolling: Obama is Hosting 'Hoodlums' in 'The Hizzouse,'" *Media Matters.org* (June 11, 2011), http://mediamatters.org/blog/201106110002

". . . Bolling's prior remarks that Obama should stop 'chugging forties' in Ireland" is from "Fox's Bolling: 'Obama is Chugging 40s in Ireland,'" *Media Matters.org* (May 23, 2011), http://mediamatters.org/blog/201105230043

Pages 65–66
That Donald Trump questioned President Obama's academic credentials is from Maggie Haberman, "Donald Trump: 'How did Barack Obama Get into Ivies?'" *Politico.com* (April 25, 2011), www.politico.com/news/stories/0411/53694.html

Page 66
That Donald Trump supported McCain-Palin in 2008 is from "Trump Endorses McCain," *CNN Politics*, September 18, 2008, http://politicalticker.blogs.cnn.com/2008/09/18/trump-endorses-mccain/

That John McCain and Sarah Palin were lousy college students is from "John McCain's GPA and College Records," *EDU In*

Review (October, 2008), www.eduinreview.com/blog/2008/10/
john-mccains-gpa-and-college-records/; and Peter Robison,
"Palin, 'Average' Student at 5 Schools, Prayed, Planned for TV,"
Bloomberg.com (September 7, 2008), www.bloomberg.com/apps/ne
ws?pid=newsarchive&sid=aYY9hiQdr5E4&refer=home

Page 67

For the poll that found high levels of admitted racial bias even
among white Democrats who intended to vote for Barack Obama,
see Ron Fournier and Trevor Thompson, "Poll: Racial Views Steer
Some White Dems Away from Obama," (September 20, 2008),
www.perla.org/blog/previouspostings/RacePoll.htm

Information on the ubiquity of implicit racial bias: Po Bronson
and Ashley Merryman, "See Baby Discriminate," *Newsweek/
The Daily Beast* (September 4, 2009), www.thedailybeast.
com/newsweek/2009/09/04/see-baby-discriminate.html;
"Test That Found Widespread Unconscious Bias Validated,"
Science Daily.com (June 18, 2009), www.sciencedaily.com/
releases/2009/06/090617142120.htm; Justin Levinson,
"Forgotten Racial Equality: Implicit Bias, Decision-Making
and Misremembering," *Duke Law Journal* 57 (November 2007),
http://papers.ssrn.com/sol3/papers.cfm?abstract_id=975793;
Eben Harrell, "Study: Racial Attitudes are Still Ingrained,
Time.com (January 8, 2009), www.time.com/time/health/
article/0,8599,1870408,00.html; Shankar Vedantam, "How the
Unconscious Mind Can Act Out Our Prejudices," *Alternet.
org* (February 18, 2010), www.alternet.org/books/145699/
how_the_unconscious_mind_can_act_out_our_prejudices_

That the media overrepresents blacks in stories about crime,
relative to their share of offenders is from Lori Dorfman and
Vincent Schiraldi, *Off Balance: Youth, Race and Crime in the News*
(Building Blocks for Youth, April 2001), www.cclp.org/documents/
BBY/offbalance.pdf

Page 68

That viewing news stories about crime reinforces false and racist beliefs about blacks is from "Negative Perception of Blacks Rises With More News Watching, Studies Say," *Science Daily.com* (July 17, 2008), www.sciencedaily.com/releases/2008/07/080717134527.htm

". . . when whites are hooked up to brain scan imaging machines and exposed even to subliminal images of black men, flashed on a screen for mere milliseconds, roughly nine in ten show dramatically increased activity in the part of the brain that is activated when a person is afraid" is from Joe Feagin, *Systemic Racism* (NY: Routledge, 2006), p. 26.

That whites are four to five times more likely to be criminally victimized by another white person than by a black person is evident from data in Michael R. Rand and Jayne E. Robinson, *Criminal Victimization in the United States, 2008 Statistical Tables*. (United States Department of Justice, Bureau of Justice Statistics, May 12, 2011), Tables 42, 48. http://bjs.ojp.usdoj.gov/content/pub/pdf/cvus0802.pdf.

". . . in one classic study, groups of whites were shown a video in which two men—one black and one white—were arguing. When the white man . . . shoved the black man at the end of the argument, only 17 percent of whites . . . said they perceived the act as violent; but when the black actor administered the shove, three of four whites said they perceived the act as a violent one" is from Birt L. Duncan, "Differential Social Perception and Attributes of Intergroup Violence: Testing the Lower Limits of Stereotyping of Blacks," *Journal of Personality and Social Psychology* (1976).

Pages 68–69
Recent research confirming that black children internalize negative images of blackness is from "Study: White and black children biased toward lighter skin," CNN.com (May 14, 2010), www.cnn.com/2010/US/05/13/doll.study/index.html

Pages 75
Information on pre-election racism aimed at the prospects of an Obama presidency can be found at, http://trailblazersblog.

dallasnews.com/archives/2008/06/stick-a-pin-in-it.html; and
http://topdocumentaryfilms.com/right-america-feeling-wronged/

Pages 81–82

". . . black folks . . . are far more optimistic about the future than
we are. Whites, despite our ongoing advantages relative to the
black and brown, are the most pessimistic of all racial groups in the
nation" is from Ronald Brownstein, "The White Working Class:
The Most Pessimistic Group in America," *The Atlantic.com* (May 27,
2011), www.theatlantic.com/politics/archive/2011/05/the-white-
working-class-the-most-pessimistic-group-in-america/239584/;
Jon Cohen and Dan Balz, "Poll: Whites without college degrees
especially pessimistic about the economy," *Washington Post.com*
(February 22, 2011), www.washingtonpost.com/wp-dyn/content/
article/2011/02/22/AR2011022200005.html; Jim Tankersley, Ron
Fournier and Nancy Cook, "Why Whites are More Pessimistic
About Their Future Than Minorities," *The Atlantic.com* (October
7, 2011), www.theatlantic.com/business/archive/2011/10/
why-whites-are-more-pessimistic-about-their-future-than-
minorities/246366/

Page 82

The *Newsweek* article on "beached white males," was Tony Dokupil,
"Dead Suit Walking," *Newsweek/The Daily Beast.com* (April 17,
2011), www.thedailybeast.com/newsweek/2011/04/17/dead-suit-
walking.html

Page 83

". . . Harvard study . . . discovered that most of us actually think . . .
that discrimination against us is more common than discrimination
against people of color" is from "Regarding Racism: Whites Think
They are the New Blacks," *Gothamist.com* (May 25, 2011), http://
gothamist.com/2011/05/25/racism_is_white_the_new_black.php;
Gregory Rodriguez, "The Unhappy White Majority," *Charlotte
Observer.com* (from the Los Angeles Times) (June 4, 2011), www.
charlotteobserver.com/2011/06/04/2348917/the-unhappy-white-
majority.html; Joan Walsh, "When Whites Say 'What About

Me?'" *Salon.com* (May 26, 2011), www.salon.com/2011/05/26/are_whites_facing_more_racism/

Pages 83–84

Information on the paucity of "minority scholarships," as a share of scholarship dollars is from U.S. General Accounting Office, "Information on Minority Targeted Scholarships," B251634. (Washington, DC: U.S. Government Printing Office, January 1994); see also Mark Katrnowitz, *The Distribution of Grants and Scholarships by Race* (September 2, 2011), www.finaid.org/scholarships/20110902racescholarships.pdf

Page 84

That only about 3.5 percent of students of color receive any kind of "minority"-related scholarship is from Stephen L. Carter, "Color-Blind and Color-Active," *The Recorder*, January 3, 1992.

Page 85

That Glenn Beck claimed President Obama "hates white people" is from "Beck: Obama has 'exposed himself as a guy' with a 'deep-seated hatred for white people,'" *Media Matters.org* (July 28, 2009), http://mediamatters.org/mmtv/200907280008

Limbaugh's comment about President Obama modeling himself after Robert Mugabe is from "Limbaugh Says Obama's Economic 'Role Model' Is Robert Mugabe, Who 'Took the White People's Farms,'" *Media Matters.org* (August 4, 2011), http://mediamatters.org/mmtv/201108040018

Pages 85–86

That Limbaugh accused Colin Powell of supporting Obama out of racial bonding is from "Limbaugh responds to Price: says all Dems 'had to do was nominate an African-American and [they've] got Colin Powell,'" *Media Matters.org* (May 18, 2009), http://mediamatters.org/mmtv/200905180025.

Page 86

Information on the attempt by the right to accuse ACORN of voter fraud, and the ridiculous nature of the allegations, is from "Dick Morris baselessly accused ACORN of 'committing voter fraud,'" *Media Matters.org* http://mediamatters.org/research/200810150013; Brad Friedman, "So Where's the ACORN Voter Fraud?" *The Brad Blog* (October 14, 2008), www.bradblog.com/?p=6512

Pages 86–87
Information on the attempts by the right to blame the Community Reinvestment Act for the housing and financial crisis (and the ridiculous nature of those charges) is from Rick Perlstein, "Mythbusting the Right's Subprime Excuses," (Campaign for America's Future, April 11, 2008), www.ourfuture.org/blog-entry/mythbusting-rights-subprime-excuses; Andy Birkey, "Bachmann: Blaming minority lending for economic crisis 'does not mean I'm a racist,'" *Minnesota Independent* (September 29, 2008), http://minnesotaindependent.com/10758/bachmann-blaming-minority-lending-for-economic-crisis-does-not-mean-im-a-racist; "Don't Blame CRA (The Sequel)," *Wall Street Journal* (December 4, 2008), http://blogs.wsj.com/economics/2008/12/04/dont-blame-cra-the-sequel/; David Abromowitz, "Defending the CRA" (Center for American Progress, November 20, 2008), www.americanprogress.org/issues/2008/11/defending_cra.html; Sara Robinson, "11 Racist Lies Conservatives Tell to Avoid Blaming Wall Street for the Financial Crisis," *Alternet.org* (October 2, 2008), www.alternet.org/story/101127/11_racist_lies_conservatives_tell_to_avoid_blaming_wall_street_for_the_financial_crisis/

". . . it was independent mortgage brokers (not even covered by the CRA) who made most of the risky loans that went bad during this period" is also from the sources cited in the preceding note.

". . . only one of the top twenty-five subprime lenders in the nation was required to follow the CRA's strictures" is from David Goldstein and Kevin Hall, "Private sector loans, not Fannie or Freddie, triggered crisis," *McClatchydc.com* (October 12, 2008), www.mcclatchydc.com/2008/10/12/53802/private-sector-loans-not-fannie.html#ixzz12xTyWY91A; and that "only 6 percent of all subprime loan dollars were loaned by CRA-covered banks to low-income people whom the law was intended to help" is from "CRA Myth vs. Fact," www.expandcra.com/about-cra/cra-myth-vs.-fact/

Page 88

". . . loans made under the aegis of CRA have tended to perform better and have lower rates of default and foreclosure than more traditional loans" is from "The WSJ News Pages Weigh In: Don't Blame the CRA" (December 30, 2008), http://delong.typepad.com/sdj/2008/12/the-wsj-news-pages-weigh-in-dont-blame-cra-the-sequel.html

". . . one recent study in Louisville discovered [that] a disproportionate number of the houses that went into foreclosure in largely black urban areas were actually owned by whites in the suburbs and were engaging in real estate speculation" is from John I. Gilderbloom, "Speculators, Not CRA, Behind Foreclosures in Black Neighborhoods," *American Banker.com* (September 7, 2011), www.americanbanker.com/bankthink/CRA--white-investors-flippers-forceclosure-black-neighborhoods-louisville-1041971-1.html?zkPrintable=true

That the deregulation of mortgage markets was largely to blame for the meltdown is from Paul Krugman, "The Gramm Connection" (March 29, 2008), http://krugman.blogs.nytimes.com/2008/03/29/the-gramm-connection/; Marcus Baram, "Who's Whining Now? Gramm Slammed by Economists," *ABC News.com* (September 19, 2008), http://abcnews.go.com/print?id=5835269

Page 89

That the originate-to-distribute model of mortgage brokering contributed to the crisis by insulating mortgage brokers from risk is from Amiyatosh Purnanandam, "Originate-to- Distribute Model and the Subprime Mortgage Crisis," April 15, 2009, http://webuser.bus.umich.edu/amiyatos/subprime_march09.pdf; "Study: Originate-to-Distribute Model to Blame for Mortgage Crisis," www.thetruthaboutmortgage.com/study-originate-to-distribute-model-to-blame-for-mortgage-crisis/

Page 90

That the right has accused President Obama of plotting a Nazi-like takeover or enslaving Americans is from Victoria Jackson, "The 3 Scariest Things About Obama," *WorldNetDaily* (July 15, 2011), www.wnd.com/?pageId=322057; "Nazi Like Concentration Camps in America" (February 3, 2009), http://freedomarizona.wordpress.com/2009/02/03/nazi-like-concentration-camps-in-america/; Sher Zieve, "Obama continues mad dash towards enslaving American people," *RenewAmerica.com* (November 13, 2009), www.renewamerica.com/columns/zieve/091113; Rush Limbaugh, "Obama to Enslave U.S. Military to Protect Abortion Funding," *FreeRepublic.com* (April 8, 2011), www.freerepublic.com/focus/news/2701949/posts; and, www.zazzle.com/obama_enslaving_america_tshirt-235575065379338404; and, "Obamacon's Enslave America," *Campaign for Liberty* (December 22, 2009) www.campaignforliberty.com/blog.php?view=30671; "Hannity Guest Compares Obama Administration's Policies to Nazism," *Huffington Post.com* (August 24, 2009), www.huffingtonpost.com/2009/08/24/hannity-guest-compares-ob_n_267804.html

"Rush Limbaugh . . . has compared the Obama health care logo to the Nazi swastika and claims that Hitler, 'ruled by dictate,' just 'like Barack Obama,'" is from "Rush Limbaugh's Obsession With Nazi Comparisons," *Media Matters.org* (August 7, 2009), http://mediamatters.org/blog/200908070035; "Limbaugh: "Adolph Hitler, like Obama, also ruled by dictate," *Media Matters.org* (August 6, 2009), http://mediamatters.org/mmtv/200908060021

That Glenn Beck has compared President Obama's proposed volunteer service corps to the Nazi SS or Nazi Youth is from "Beck claims Obama's 'civilian national security force' is 'what Hitler did with the SS,' 'what Saddam Hussein' did," *Media Matters.org* (August 27, 2009), http://mediamatters.org/mmtv/200908270036

Page 91

Bill O'Reilly's claim about the nomination of Sonia Sotomayor to the Supreme Court being evidence that the Obama administration believes "white men are the problem in America" and need to be replaced in positions of power by women and folks of color, is from Jason Linkins, "Bill O'Reilly: 'The Left Sees White Men as the Problem'" (VIDEO), *Huffington Post.com* (May 29, 2009), www.huffingtonpost.com/2009/05/29/bill-oreilly-the-left-see_n_209054.html

That Pat Buchanan suggested Sotomayor was barely literate and an affirmative action appointment is from "Buchanan declares Sotomayor an 'affirmative action pick,'" *Media Matters.org* (May 26, 2009), http://mediamatters.org/mmtv/200905260066

Limbaugh's comparison of Sotomayor to David Duke is from "Limbaugh: Nominating Sotomayor Like Nominating David Duke," *Huffington Post.com* (May 29, 2009), www.huffingtonpost.com/2009/05/29/limbaugh-nominating-sotom_n_209151.html

Pages 91–92
Limbaugh's claim that the only way to get a job in the Obama Administration is by "hating white people" is from "Rush Limbaugh: President Obama Hates White People," *DailyKosTV* (May 29, 2009), www.dailykostv.com/w/001800/

Page 92
Claims by right-wing commentators that a proposed tax on tanning bed customers was evidence of the Obama Administration's anti-white racism: from "Beck sub Thompson: Tanning tax makes health bill 'racist' because 'dark-skinned people' don't use tanning salons," *Media Matters.org* (March 30, 2010), http://mediamatters.org/mmtv/201003300011; "Quinn: Tanning tax is a 'race-based tax' from 'the most racist administration . . . since Woodrow Wilson,'" *Media Matters.org* (July 6, 2010), http://mediamatters.org/mmtv/201007060006

Page 93
That Lou Dobbs claimed Mexicans were seeking to reconquer the Southwest United States and spreading leprosy throughout the country is from "Lou Dobbs Tonight" (March 31, 2006), http://edition.cnn.com/TRANSCRIPTS/0603/31/ldt.01.html

That Dobbs' claims are disproved by CDC data is from "CBS Contributor Dobbs defends false leprosy claim after confrontation by CBS' Stahl," *Media Matters.org* (May 11, 2007), http://mediamatters.org/research/200705110004

That conservative commentators blamed Mexican immigrants for swine flu is from "Hey, maybe we'll finally get serious about borders now; Update: 2 swine flu cases confirmed in Kansas; 8 probable in NYC; Update: US declares public health emergency," *Michelle Malkin.com* (April 25, 2009), http://michellemalkin.com/2009/04/25/hey-maybe-well-finally-get-serious-about-borders-now/; "Paranoia Pandemic: Conservative media baselessly blame swine flu outbreak on immigrants," *Media Matters.org* (April 27, 2009), http://mediamatters.org/research/200904270037

That Mexicans were not to blame for swine flu is from Jon Cohen, "Exclusive Interview: CDC Head Virus Sleuth," *Science Insider* (April 29, 2009), http://news.sciencemag.org/scienceinsider/2009/04/exclusive-cdc-h.html; Tom Philpott, "'New Scientist': Swine flu stems from virus that evolved in U.S.," *Grist.org* (April 30, 2009), www.grist.org/article/2009-04-30-NS-swine-cafos

Page 94

That immigration (including undocumented migration) stimulates the economy more than it results in an outflow of dollars via social services is from Chris Isidore, "Illegal Workers: Good for U.S. Economy," *CNN Money* (May 1, 2006), http://money.cnn.com/2006/05/01/news/economy/immigration_economy/index.htm; Angela M. Kelley, "The Economic Impact of Immigration," *Immigration Daily* (January 7, 2008), www.ilw.com/articles/2008,0107-kelley.shtml

That NAFTA is largely to blame for increased migration from Mexico is from Dustin Ensinger, "Illegal Immigration and NAFTA," *Economy in Crisis* (February 5, 2011), http://economyincrisis.org/content/illegal-immigration-and-nafta; Roger Bybee and Carolyn Winter, "Immigration Flood Unleashed by NAFTA's Disastrous Impact on Mexican Economy," *Common Dreams.org* (April 25,

2006), www.commondreams.org/views06/0425-30.htm; "NAFTA and Illegal Immigration," *Economist's View* (July 1, 2006), http://economistsview.typepad.com/economistsview/2006/07/nafta_and_illeg.html

Page 98

That the much maligned Ethnic Studies program in the Tucson Unified School District has boosted Latino student performance is from *Save Ethnic Studies, Data Analysis and Evaluation* (2011), http://saveethnicstudies.org/assets/docs/proven_results/Save_Ethnic_Studies_Data_Analysis_and_Evaluation.pdf; and for information on the overall benefits of Ethnic Studies courses, see Christine E. Sleeter, "The Academic and Social Value of Ethnic Studies: A Research Review," (Washington, DC: National Education Association, 2011), http://saveethnicstudies.org/assets/docs/proven_results/Academinc-and-social-value-of-ethnic-studies.pdf

Page 99

"Pat Buchanan's lament that 'traditional Americans' are losing 'their' country" is from Liliana Segura, "Pat Buchanan's Latest Racist Rant: 'Traditional Americans are Losing Their Nation," *Alternet. org* (October 21, 2009), www.alternet.org/blogs/rights/143405/pat_buchanan's_latest_racist_rant%3A_%22traditional_americans_are_losing_their_nation%22/

Page 100

"Michelle Bachmann . . . recently bragged about growing up in 'John Wayne's America,'" is from "Michelle Bachmann: Washington Is 'Corrupt Paradigm' and I'll Change It," *NewsMax.com* (June 26, 2011), www.newsmax.com/InsideCover/michele-bachmann-cbs-fox/2011/06/26/id/401506

Glenn Beck's weepy presentation of the two nostalgic commercials was from "Glenn Beck Cries AGAIN on Air, Pining for a Simpler Time in America," *Huffington Post.com* (October 15, 2009), www.huffingtonpost.com/2009/10/15/glenn-beck-cries-again-on_n_323197.html

Page 102

That Dr. Martin Luther King Jr. called the United States the "greatest purveyor of violence in the world today" is from Rev. Martin Luther King Jr., "Beyond Vietnam: A Time to Break Silence" (April 4, 1967), speech at Riverside Church, NYC, www. hartford-hwp.com/archives/45a/058.html

Page 103

That John Wayne got out of military service to further his movie career is from Glenn Greenwald, *Great American Hypocrites: Toppling the Big Myths of Republican Politics*. (NY: Crown Books, 2008), www. amazon.com/exec/obidos/ASIN/0307408027/crooksandliar-20/ ref=nosim/

Page 105

That Michelle Bachmann claimed, ignorantly, that the founding fathers had worked "tirelessly" to end enslavement, is from Sahil Kapur, "Bachmann: Founding fathers 'worked tirelessly' to end slavery," *The Raw Story* (January 25, 2011), www.rawstory.com/rs/2011/01/25/ bachmann-founding-fathers-worked-tirelessly-slavery/

That the GOP excised all references to slavery when reading the Constitution on the House floor, after taking control of the chamber in the 111th Congress, is from Elizabeth B. Wydra "Why did the GOP 'edit' the Constitution?" *Huffington Post.com* (January 6, 2011), www.huffingtonpost.com/elizabeth-b-wydra/ why-did-the-gop-edit-the_b_805224.html; Greg Sargent, "Huck Finning the Constitution," *Washington Post.com* (January 6, 2011), http://voices.washingtonpost.com/plum-line/2011/01/huck_ finning_the_constitution.html; Robert McNamara, "Censoring the Constitution and Mark Twain," http://history1800s.about. com/b/2011/01/07/censoring-the-constitution-and-mark-twain. htm; Evan McMorris-Santoro, "House Reading Amended Slavery-Free Constitution This Morning," *Talking Points Memo* (January 6, 2011), http://tpmdc.talkingpointsmemo.com/2011/01/house-reading-amended-slavery-free-constitution.php

Page 106

That Bachmann said the founders fashioned a republic where everyone was equal, without regard to color, is from Bob Cesca, "Super Stupid," *Bob Cesca's Awesome Blog* (January 25, 2011), http://bobcesca.com/blog-archives/2011/01/super_stupid_57.html

That Glenn Beck said George Washington "loved the Indians" is from "Glenn Beck Failed His 40-Day Challenge," *Media Matters.org* (October 29, 2010), http://mediamatters.org/research/201010290040

"Washington wrote to Major General John Sullivan, imploring him to 'lay waste' to all Iroquois settlements, so that their lands may not be 'merely overrun but destroyed,'" is from Johannah Cornblatt, "'Town Destroyer' Versus the Iroquois Indians," *U.S. News and World Report* (June 27, 2008), www.usnews.com/news/national/articles/2008/06/27/town-destroyer-versus-the-iroquois-indians; "Sullivan Expedition," http://en.wikipedia.org/wiki/Sullivan_Expedition

Pages 107–108

That Elena Kagan was attacked by the right for concurring with Thurgood Marshall's opinion that the Constitution had been "defective from the start" due to enslavement, is from "Limbaugh attacks Thurgood Marshall for view that original Constitution which allowed slavery was 'defective,'" *Media Matters.org* (May 10, 2010), http://mediamatters.org/mmtv/201005100049, and "Limbaugh: Elena Kagan and Thurgood Marshall look at 'me and people like me as the oppressors,'" *Media Matters.org* (May 10, 2010), http://mediamatters.org/mmtv/201005100047; "Republicans Defend Slavery to Attack Kagan," *PERRspectives* (May 10, 2010), www.perrspectives.com/blog/archives/001855.htm

Page 108

"Santorum recently bellowed on the campaign trail, America was a 'great place before 1965,'" is from "Rick Santorum: 'America Was a Great Country Before 1965,'" *Crooks and Liars.*

com (June 5, 2011), http://videocafe.crooksandliars.com/heather/rick-santorum-america-was-great-country-19

Page 109
"Mike Huckabee . . . criticized the president for 'not seeing America' the way 'we do,' and specifically because while Obama was living in places like Indonesia for a brief period, or Hawaii (doing God knows what), 'we' were going to Boy Scout and Rotary Club meetings" is from Eric Hananoki, "Huckabee Explains Obama's 'Different Worldview': 'Our Communities Were Filled With Rotary Clubs, Not Madrassas,'" *Media Matters.org* (March 2, 2011), http://mediamatters.org/blog/201103020040

Page 114
Data on the tax rates in 1957 is from *Federal Individual Income Tax Rates History, Income Years 1913-2011*, The Tax Foundation, www.taxfoundation.org/files/fed_individual_rate_history-20110323.pdf

That the corporate tax burden was higher in the 1950s than it is today is from Robert McIntyre and T.D. Coo Nguyen, "The Gap Between Statutory and Real Corporate Tax Rates," *Multinational Monitor*, 25:11 (2005), http://reclaimdemocracy.org/corporate_welfare/real_tax_rates_plummet.php; Donald Barlett and James Steele, "Tax Times Are Corporations Paying Their Share?" *What Went Wrong?* (April 16, 2011), http://americawhatwentwrong. org/story/taxes-and-corporations/, Barry Ritholtz, "Corporate Tax Rates, Then and Now," *The Big Picture* (April 14, 2011), www.ritholtz.com/blog/2011/04/corporate-tax-rates-then-and-now/; Eric Toder, "Is the Corporate Tax Going Away?" *Christian Science Monitor* (April 27, 2011), www.csmonitor.com/Business/Tax-VOX/2011/0427/Is-the-corporate-tax-going-away

Page 116
". . . the Homestead Act, passed in 1862 . . . gave over 200 million acres of essentially 'free' land to white families," is from Joe Feagin, "Toward and Integrated Theory of Systemic Racism," in *The Changing Terrain of Race and Ethnicity*, eds., Maria Krysan and Amanda E. Lewis (NY: Russell Sage Foundation, 2004), 213–214.

Page 117

Information on the size, scope and racial exclusivity of the FHA and VA loans is from Massey and Denton, 1993 (previously cited: see page 31); also Melvin Oliver and Thomas Shapiro, *Black Wealth/White Wealth: A New Perspective on Racial Inequality* (NY: Routledge, 1996).

Page 118

That FDR had to capitulate to racist demands to exclude blacks from the New Deal in order to get social safety net programs passed, is from David M. Kennedy, *Freedom From Fear: The American People in Depression and War, 1929–1945* (Oxford, 1999).

Pages 118–119

That the GI Bill benefits were racially discriminatory in application and receipt is from Dena Roth, "It's Not the Diversity Stupid: The Case for Affirmative Action," *The Current* (December 2005), www.columbia.edu/cu/current/articles/roth.html; "The GI Bill Was Affirmative Action for Poor Whites" *The Devil's Advocate* (October 7, 2010), http://dissention.wordpress.com/2010/10/07/the-gi-bill-was-affirmative-action-for-poor-whites/; Ira Katznelson, "When Affirmative Action Was White," (Poverty and Race Research Action Council, *Poverty and Race*, March/April, 2006), www.prrac.org/full_text.php?text_id=1065&item_id=9751&newsletter_id=86&header=Race+%2F+Racism

Page 119

That early rationales for cash welfare included the desire to help white women escape paid labor and stay home to care for their children is from John J. Siegfried, *Better Living Through Economics* (Cambridge: Harvard University Press, 2010), p. 131; Bridgette Baldwin, "Stratification of the Welfare Poor: Intersections of Gender, Race, and 'Worthiness' in Poverty Discourse and Policy," *The Modern American* (Spring 2010); http://digitalcommons.wcl.american.edu/cgi/viewcontent.cgi?article=1002&context=tma; and Kenneth Neubeck and Noel Cazenave, *Welfare Racism: Playing the Race Card Against America's Poor* (NY: Routledge, 2002)

Page 120

". . . antipoverty efforts had helped bring down poverty rates by roughly half between 1960 and 1973, and by a third in just the first eight years of the Great Society programs," is from DeNavas-Walt, Proctor and Smith, 2010 (previously cited: see page 44), Tables B-2 and B-3, pp. 62, 68.

Page 123–126

Information on the Nottoway Plantation and the Randolph family is from www.nottoway.com/html/nottoway-plantation-history.htm; and M.R. Ailenroc, *The White Castle of Louisiana*, www.amazon.com/White-Castle-Lousiana-M-Ailenroc/dp/B003SH0DV8

Page 126

Information on the *bracero* program is from http://en.wikipedia.org/wiki/Bracero_Program

Page 127

"Ninety percent of the labor used to build the Central Pacific Railroad in the 1860s was Chinese" is from http://cprr.org/Museum/Chinese_Laborers.html; Christopher Clark and Nancy Hewitt, Herbert Gutman and the American Social History Project. *Who Built America? Working People and the Nation's History to 1877* (St. Martin's Press, 2000).

"Each year, African Americans alone spend over $700 billion with white-owned companies" is from *Sacramento Observer* (August 11, 2004), www.highbeam.com/doc/1P1-99959704.html (which notes an anticipated annual consumer clout for blacks of around $965 billion by 2009, up from $723 billion at the time of the article), and Ollie A. Johnson III and Karin L. Stanford, eds., *Black Political Organizations in the Post–Civil Rights Era* (Rutgers University Press, 2002), p. 167 (which notes that only about 7 percent of African American purchases are directed to black owned businesses).

That incarceration transfers money from urban communities of color to rural white communities is from Sarah Lawrence and Jeremy Travis, *The New Landscape of Imprisonment: Mapping America's Prison Expansion* (Washington, DC: Urban Institute, April

2004), www.urban.org/UploadedPDF/410994_mapping_prisons. pdf; Christian Smith-Socaris, "Prisoners of the Census: How the Incarcerated Are Counted Distorts Our Politics" (Progressive States Network, September 14, 2009), www.progressivestates.org/ news/dispatch/prisoners-the-census-how-the-incarcerated-are-counted-distorts-our-politics

Page 130

Information on predatory mortgage lending in the 1990s is from Michael Hudson, *Merchants of Misery: How Corporate America Profits from Poverty* (Common Courage Press: 1996), www.amazon.com/ Merchants-Misery-Corporate-America-Profits/dp/1567510825/ ref=tmm_pap_title_0

Information on Citi's predatory practices in North Carolina is from "Special Report: Banking on Misery – Citigroup, Wall Street and the Fleecing of the South," *Facing South* 51 (June 5, 2003).

Pages 130–131

Historic information on redlining can be found in Massey and Denton, 1993 (previously cited: see page 31).

Pages 131–132

". . . folks in middle-class and mostly white counties like Suffolk and Nassau, on Long Island, are now facing higher foreclosure rates than residents in Brooklyn or Queens" is from Derrick Henry and Janet Roberts, "Long Island Foreclosures Rise, With No End In Sight," *New York Times* (May 13, 2009), www.nytimes.com/2009/05/17/ nyregion/long-island/17mortli.html?pagewanted=all; Courtney Allen, "Foreclosures 40% Higher in Long Island," *Foreclosure Warehouse.com* www.foreclosurewarehouse.com/content/ foreclosures/foreclosure-rates/foreclosures-40-higher-in-long-island/; Heather Hill Cernoc, "One in 10 NYC Mortgages Seriously Delinquent," *DSNews.com* (June 28, 2011), www. dsnews.com/articles/one-in-10-nyc-mortgages-seriously-delinquent-2011-06-28. For additional information on the spread of the foreclosure crisis : "Foreclosure Crisis Worsens in Most U.S.

Metros," *Fox News.com* (October 28, 2010), www.foxnews.com/us/2010/10/28/foreclosure-crisis-worsens-metros/

Page 133

". . . the reason the United States has such a feeble social safety net—a weak system of unemployment insurance, limited cash-based support, paltry food subsidies and limited public health care initiatives—is due to the perception on the part of large numbers of us that black folks will abuse such programs" is from Martin Gilens, "'Race Coding' and White Opposition to Welfare," *American Political Science Review* (1996), 593–595; Alberto Alesina, Edward Glaeser, and Bruce Sacerdote, *Why Doesn't the U.S. Have a European-Style Welfare State?* (Harvard Institute of Economic Research, Discussion Paper No. 1933, November 2001), http://post.economics.harvard.edu/hier/2001papers/2001list.html. For Martin Gilens' book-length analysis of the role of racial imagery on public perceptions of "welfare" programs: www.amazon.com/Why-Americans-Hate-Welfare-Communication/dp/0226293653/ref=sr_1_1?ie=UTF8&s=books&qid=1249928092&sr=1-1

Page 134

For Jill Quadagno's analysis of how racism has undermined anti-poverty efforts: www.amazon.com/Color-Welfare-Racism-Undermined-Poverty/dp/0195101227//ref=pd_sim_b_2

For Neubeck and Cazenave's analysis of how racism has undermined antipoverty initiatives: www.amazon.com/Welfare-Racism-Playing-Against-Americas/dp/0415923417/ref=sr_1_1?ie=UTF8&s=books&qid=1249928165&sr=1-1

". . . a comprehensive comparison of various social programs in the U.S. and Europe found that racial hostility to people of color better explains opposition to high levels of social spending here than any other economic or political variable" is from Alesina, Glaeser and Sacerdote, 2001 (previously cited: see page 133).

Page 137

". . . corporate America is hoarding over $2 trillion in cash reserves—and banks are hoarding trillions more" is from John

Aidan Byrne, "U.S. Firms Hoarding $2 Trillion," *New York Post* (August 6, 2011), www.nypost.com/p/news/business/hoarding_cash_Yzfk2c8aK1wAPrZCRdEVnJ; Rich Blake and Dahlia Fahmy, "Hoarding, Not Hiring Corporations Stockpile Mountains of Cash," *ABC News* (April 1, 2010), http://abcnews.go.com/Business/hoarding-hiring-corporations-stockpile-mountain-cash/story?id=10250559; Ben Casselman and Justin Lahart, "Companies Shun Investment, Hoard Cash," *Wall Street Journal* (September 17, 2011), http://online.wsj.com/article/SB10001424053111903927204576574720017009568.html

Page 138

"Corporate profitability is at its highest point in fifty years" is from Catherine Rampell, "Corporate Profits Were the Highest on Record Last Quarter," *New York Times* (November 23, 2010), www.nytimes.com/2010/11/24/business/economy/24econ.html

". . . 90 percent of the nation's recent income growth has gone to corporate profits (while only about one-tenth of one percent went to worker wages)" is from "Since 2009, 88 Percent of Income Growth Went to Corporate Profits, Just One Percent Went to Wages," *Think Progress.org* (June 30, 2011), http://thinkprogress.org/economy/2011/06/30/258388/corporate-profits-recovery/: "

Page 140

Newt Gingrich's comment about the immorality of unemployment benefits is from Sam Stein, "Florida GOP Debate: Newt Gingrich Blasts 99ers Over Unemployment Insurance," *Huffington Post.com* (September 22, 2011), www.huffingtonpost.com/2011/09/22/florida-gop-debate-newt-gingrich-99ers-unemmployed_n_977059.html. For an additional conservative critique of unemployment benefits: Alan Pyke, "Rep. Steve King: Unemployment Benefits Have Created 'A Nation of Slackers,'" *Political Correction* (September 16, 2011), http://politicalcorrection.org/blog/201109160005

Pages 140–141

Information on Rick Santelli's "rant heard round the world" is from "Rick Santelli's Shout Heard 'Round the World," *CNBC.com* (February 22, 2009), www.cnbc.com/id/29283701/Rick_Santelli_s_ Shout_Heard_Round_the_World; Eric Etheridge, "Rick Santelli: Tea Party Time," *New York Times Opinionator* (February 20, 2009), http://opinionator.blogs.nytimes.com/2009/02/20/rick-santelli-tea-party-time/; Paul Bedard, "Rick Santelli Gets Credit for Tea Party Movement," *U.S. News and World Report* (January 25, 2010), www.usnews.com/news/blogs/washington-whispers/2010/01/25/rick-santelli-gets-credit-for-tea-party-movement

Page 150 et seq.

Information on white allies can be found at www.timwise.org/reading-list/; and in Herbert Aptheker, *Anti-Racism in U.S. History: The First Two Hundred Years*, www.amazon.com/Anti-Racism-U-S-History-Contributions-American/dp/0275948080/ref=sr_1_1?s=books&ie=UTF8&qid=1281354845&sr=1-1Herbert.

Page 153

The closing quote is from James Baldwin, *Nobody Knows My Name* (Dell Publishing, 1963)

 Tim Wise is among the nation's most prominent writers and educators on issues of racial justice. He is the author of five previous books on racism and has contributed essays or chapters to more than twenty additional volumes. Wise has spoken to more than a million people on more than 750 college and high school campuses across the United States, and has trained teachers, employers, nonprofit agencies, physicians and others on methods of dismantling racism in their institutions. He has appeared on hundreds of radio and television programs to discuss racial issues, and his writings are taught in colleges and universities worldwide. Wise lives in Nashville with his wife and two daughters.

OTHER BOOKS BY TIM WISE

Colorblind: The Rise of Post-Racial Politics and the Retreat from Racial Equity (Open Media Series / City Lights Books, 2010)

Between Barack and a Hard Place: Racism and White Denial in the Age of Obama (Open Media Series / City Lights Books, 2009)

Speaking Treason Fluently: Anti-Racist Reflections from an Angry White Male (Soft Skull Press, 2008)

White Like Me: Reflections on Race from a Privileged Son (Soft Skull Press, 2005, revised 2008)

Affirmative Action: Racial Preference in Black and White (Routledge, 2005)